ARTES LATINAE

LATIN
SELF-TEACHING

Teacher's Guide to Unit Tests for Level One

by
Waldo E. Sweet
and
Judith B. Moore

Bolchazy-Carducci Publishers, Inc.
Wauconda, Illinois

Bolchazy-Carducci Publishers, Inc.
1000 Brown Street, Unit 101
Wauconda, IL 60084
WWW.BOLCHAZY.COM

Printed in the United States of America
2005
by United Graphics

ISBN 0-86516-298-0

TABLE OF CONTENTS

PAGE

TABLE OF CONTENTS—TESTS

INTRODUCTION TO TESTING

Function of Tests. A test serves several functions:
1) It informs the teacher of the student's achievement.
2) It informs the student of his own achievement.
3) It motivates the student to do his work thoroughly.
4) By studying for a test and taking it, the student often synthesizes what he has learned.
5) It gives more exposure to the language.

It would seem desirable to try to teach the students to regard tests as diagnostic, something designed to help them discover whether they are ready for the next Unit. Tests offer a fine opportunity for teaching which is often overlooked: here is a time when the student is particularly ready to be helped.

The Unit Tests for *Latin: Level One* contain multiple questions of a similar nature for each area studied, as well as review. There are questions on current and review Basic Sentences, paradigms, Question-and-Answer items, and, beginning with Unit 16, sight passages.

On the whole, students with the lowest error rate in *Latin: Level One* will score highest in the tests, but there will be exceptions in almost every class. Student A goes through 400 frames and makes 10 errors. He takes no corrective action and unless the program drills further on these particular points, he may not know them. Student B makes 20 errors in 400 frames, but whenever he makes an error he takes it upon himself to learn the point which he has just missed.

Achievement Spread. The teacher should be warned that *Latin: Level One* does not *reduce* the difference in achievement between students but rather *increases* it. Programming makes it more obvious how great the gap can be between the fast and slow learner. However, with programmed materials, even the slower students can still learn Latin—if they spend the extra time. This may mean that slower students should repeat a part or the whole of a Unit where their performance was unsatisfactory, or otherwise strengthen their learning before they proceed to the next Unit.

As the students learn more and more and begin to do sight reading, the gaps become wider and wider. The teacher will discover that bright students will be able to read a passage at sight almost perfectly, while slower students can make almost nothing of the same passage without help.

Programming makes the achievement spread more apparent than does the traditional system of instruction. It must be constantly

i

emphasized that to compete on anything like equal terms, the slower student must be made to realize that he has to put in more time.

Some teachers will want to take time to show the slower students how to prepare properly for the tests. First, the students should thoroughly review the Basic Sentences of the particular Unit, along with the questions on these sentences. Then they should know the paradigms well. Combined with these, a review of the vocabulary items at the end of each Unit should include knowing the meaning of each word as it is used in a Basic Sentence. All students should be advised that regular review is essential.

Administration of Tests. First and foremost, some teachers will not have the time to administer and correct personally all the questions on all the tests for all the students. However, all the testing material which the teacher could possibly use is available to him.

If the tests are to be used to give grades, then the teacher should do the grading himself, unless skilled assistants are available. Student help is not entirely reliable because of the many instances of judgment which are required. But many of the other functions of testing may be served even if the scores are not recorded for the purpose of grading. It is not necessary to have all the tests count as regular tests.

Here are some possible procedures which may be used when scores are not recorded:
1) Tests are corrected by the students in class after they have finished the tests.
2) Tests are corrected by other students and returned to the student. It is desirable to let the students communicate as they are doing this so that each student can get information on his own performance, and also so that his grading of the other student's paper will be accurate.
3) The teacher moves around the class while the students are taking the test and gives help, makes corrections, etc.
4) Students work in groups and decide on one answer. It is important to have the groups homogeneous, so that one person doesn't supply all the answers. If there is a markedly superior student or one who is aggressive about answering, he may be used as an assistant, as in #2.
5) Students use whatever means they need to get the answer: reference to notes, peeking at a neighbor's paper, asking friends, etc. This could be called a "Cheating Test."
6) The test is done in class, question by question (written or oral), and then corrected immediately. This has the advantage of giving the student immediate feedback.
7) The test may be used as a take-home exercise to be corrected in class.

Scoring the Tests. The tests are constructed with the idea that 90% is a good performance, while 70%, though passing, indicates clearly that the test on the next Unit will be still lower unless the Unit (or parts of it) is repeated.

One difficulty in evaluating performance is that teachers differ so much in the way they mark. One recommended procedure is to make no distinction between serious and trivial errors. A word is wrong if there is any deviation: **agnī, canibus, lupōs, agnibus,** and **nōn mordet** are all equally wrong if the desired response is **lupī.**

There are a few exceptions:
1) If an answer is correct except for macrons, the student receives half credit.
2) Where there is a Latin question and answer which is not purely structural, that is, where because of the complexities of substitution, transformation, and expansion an answer requires "comprehension" of the meaning, the student receives half credit. It must be obvious that he understood the question and knew what the answer was but simply could not produce the correct Latin form.
3) The student is not penalized more than once for the same error in a series; that is, if in giving the paradigm of **auctor** the student omits the macron on the oblique forms (*auctorem** for **auctōrem** and so on), this is counted as a single error.

Here are some examples of this system of scoring. In production of Basic Sentences, paradigms, and pattern practice, each word counts two points. One point is taken off for a wrong macron (or macrons) per word; all credit is taken off if otherwise misspelled. In other words, no credit for **canem** if the correct answer was **canis,** but half credit for ***cānis.** No attempt is thus made to distinguish between important and unimportant errors, except for wrong macrons. In giving answers to Latin questions, each word counts four points. There is two points credit if the student seems to have understood the question but misspells the answer in some way. In other words, half credit is given for **canem** if the correct answer was **canis,** since the student could read the question well enough to know that some form of **canis** was required.

However, in grading, the teacher should realize that the credit for each item is only a suggested credit and that the teacher may prefer to use his own system of weighting the tests. In any event, it seems obvious that students should not be told in advance of a test how much each part counts, since that might give away the answer.

The scores on the Unit Tests, of course, will not be the only factors to take into account in the grading. Heavy weight should be given to how well the student can apply in class what he has learned in *Latin: Level One.*

It is recommended in the strongest terms that the student not be marked on his performance in *Latin: Level One* itself but on his application of what he learns.

Conversion Tables. For the convenience of the teacher, conversion tables which convert the raw scores into percentage scores have been included. The conversion tables will be found at the end of the Unit Tests. However, these tables do not include percentage scores for the Extra Readings which begin with the test for Unit 16. Suggestions for evaluating the Extra Readings are given in this Guide following the Unit 16 test.

Testing of Sight Readings. Beginning with Unit 16 there are sight passages called "Extra Readings." These may be tested in several ways. At one extreme, the student is not given the lexical meaning of any verbs or substantives. Some other part of speech, however, such as **vix** or **haud**, would usually be explained. With a sentence like **Vertit lympha rotam, rota petram, petra farīnam**, the student gets seven points (one per word) for seeing the structure, as in an answer like this, "A blanks B, B blanks C, and C blanks D," or, "A **lympha vertit**'s a **rotam**," etc. One point is given for each correct lexical item, with a bonus of three for the entire answer, making 17 points for a perfect answer. This technique needs extra drill in class. The other extreme would be to put the meaning of *all* the unknown words on the board. This seems too easy. With "turns," "water," "wheel," "millstone," and "flour," a student would not even need to look at the Latin to get the meaning.

There are three other approaches which seem feasible. One is to put on the board only a few of the meanings, just enough to get them started; e.g., the meaning of **vertit**. A second would be to give them the English derivative of some (or all) of the words, "reVERT," "ROTate," "PETRoleum," etc. A third would be to introduce some or all of these words in class earlier in the course. But whatever method is adopted, the teacher should remember that the main purpose of this reading is not to teach the meaning of **lympha** but to show the student how to solve the problem of unknown lexical items by paying close attention to the structure, the context, and English derivatives.

Scoring of Sight Readings. For giving the meaning of sight sentences, two points are given per word, one for the correct structure and one for the correct lexical meaning, plus three points bonus for getting the total meaning. Let us assume that **Hilarem datōrem dīligit Deus** was not a Basic Sentence but used as a sight sentence. The student says that this means that a cheerful giver loves God. The correct answer would be worth 11 points (four words plus the bonus of three points). This student would receive 5 points, as follows:
1) **Hilarem**: one point for right lexical meaning,
2) **datōrem**: one point for right lexical meaning,
3) **dīligit**: two points for both lexical and structural meaning,
4) **Deus**: one point for correct lexical meaning, and
5) total meaning: no credit.
The score of 5 out of 11 is a poor score, reflecting one extremely serious error, failure to distinguish subject and object.

The question may now arise what sort of credit we should grant for "A cheerful giver is loved by God." It would be our feeling that this should receive full credit. It is true that sometimes such an answer may be just a lucky guess, but if the student really can't tell subject from object or an active verb from a passive one, this fact will emerge soon enough.

As the students progress in *Latin: Level One* they will find numerous sentences where a "literal translation" is almost meaningless. The teacher should require only that the answer, if in English, be one which sounds natural and appropriate to the context.

Tests on Outside Reading. Many teachers will wish to introduce tests on outside readings much earlier than Unit 16. The copious range of the Reader will make such material for testing readily available. In general, the sentences on the Tests concentrate more on review structures than on the structures taught in the particular Unit being tested.

However, when the students do extra reading in Latin not contained in the programmed text, the teacher should test the material covered. If the students are tested on *Latin: Level One* alone, many students will learn only that and lack the experience of reading other Latin materials.

UNIT TESTS

TEST FOR UNIT 2 OF *LATIN: LEVEL ONE*

4 pts. 1) Write the Latin vowel which your teacher says:_____.

4 pts. 2) Write another Latin vowel which your teacher says:_____.

4 pts. 3) Write another Latin vowel which your teacher says:_____.

4 pts. 4) Write the Latin syllable which your teacher says:_____.

4 pts. 5) Write another Latin syllable which your teacher says:_____.

4 pts. 6) Write another Latin syllable which your teacher says:_____.

24 pts. 7) Read this sentence aloud to your teacher: **Vestis virum reddit.**

Total
48 pts.

For items 1), 2), and 3) choose from /a/, /ā/, /e/, /ē/, /i/, /ī/, /o/, /ō/, /u/, and /ū/.

For items 4), 5), and 6) choose from **ab, ob, et, at, ut, id, it, ve, va, vi,** and **vu.**

8 points per word. Check for /w/ sound in **Vestis** and **virum,** trilled /r/s in **virum** and **reddit,** and double consonant /**d**/ in **reddit.**

In the tests for Units, 2, 3, 5, and 6 the weighting of the pronunciation of the Basic Sentences must be somewhat impressionistic. Some sentences are obviously longer than others. The teacher may prefer to grade pronunciation by listening to the students as they work.

NOTE: A table to convert the students' scores to a percentage grade can be found at the end of this book.

TEST FOR UNIT 3 OF *LATIN: LEVEL ONE*

Write the Latin vowels which your teacher will pronounce. Remember: if the vowel is *long* you must add the macron.

No part credit for items 1) through 5).

4 pts.   1)   This vowel is _____ .

4 pts.   2)   This vowel is _____ .

4 pts.   3)   This vowel is _____ .

4 pts.   4)   This vowel is _____ .

4 pts.   5)   This vowel is _____ .

For items 1) through 5) the teacher can choose vowels listed for the test for Unit 2. However, if the students had any difficulty with particular vowel sounds, it would be well to include these on this test as a check.

24 pts.   6)   Read aloud the Basic Sentence which your teacher indicates:

> **Manus manum lavat.**
>
> **Hilarem datōrem dīligit Deus.**
>
> **Vēritātem diēs aperit.**

Listen particularly for:

4 short /a/s

trilled /r/, short /e/ in **Deus,** and correct stress.

short /i/ in **diēs,** trilled /r/s, correct stress, and /w/ sound in **Vēritātem.**

Total
44 pts.

NOTE: A table to convert the students' scores to a percentage grade can be found at the end of this book.

1) Write the Basic Sentence which each of these pictures illustrates. Be sure to mark the long vowels with macrons.

2 points for each word; 1 point off for wrong macron.

8 pts.   a) **El ········ n ·· c···· m····.**

Elephantus nōn capit mūrem .

8 pts.   b) **H ······ d ······ d ······ D···.**

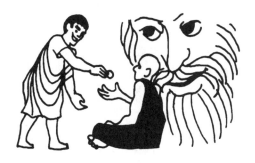

Hilarem datōrem dīligit Deus .

6 pts.   c) **M ···· m ···· l ····.**

Manus manum lavat .

6 pts. 2) In the sentence **Vēritātem diēs aperit**, the

subject is the word _____**diēs**_____ ; the

object is the word _____**Vēritātem**_____ ; and the

verb is the word _____**aperit**_____ .

4 pts. 3) Underline the *subject* in these English sentences:
a) The <u>smoke</u> went up the chimney.
b) The <u>mouse</u> was caught by the cat.

4 pts. 4) Underline the *object* in these English sentences:
a) The woman lost her <u>cat</u> in the woods.
b) The man threw his alarm <u>clock</u> out the window.

4 pts. 5) Underline the *verb* in these English sentences:
a) The boy <u>read</u> his book.
b) The stream <u>flows</u> quietly.

4 pts. 6) You were told that the most important frame of the course was one in which you learned that Latin *never* signals subject and object by the position of the words but by using the signals

{ **· s** } and { **· m** }.

8 pts. 7) Write these vowels from dictation. There will be both long and short vowels.

No credit if macron is missed.

a)_____ b)_____ c)_____ d)_____

8 pts. 8) Write these syllables from dictation. There will be both long and short vowels.

No credit if macron is missed.

Total
60 pts.

a)_____ b)_____ c)_____ d)_____

For items 7) and 8) the teacher can again refer to the lists in the notes for the test for Unit 2. This test is a final check on the students' pronunciation of individual vowels and random syllables. However, if the teacher feels that more testing is needed, he may reuse items 7) and 8) choosing other vowels and syllables.

NOTE: A table to convert the students' scores to a percentage grade can be found at the end of this book.

1) On the model of **Elephantus nōn capit mūrem**, describe these pictures to say that the important one ignores the unimportant one.

6 points per sentence. 1 point for **nōn**; 1 point for **capit**; 2 points for the subject; 2 points for the object; 1 point off for wrong macron.

6 pts.   a)   **Taurus nōn capit vulpem** _____ .

6 pts.   b)   **Leō nōn capit anum** _____ .

6 pts.   c)   **Lupus nōn capit mūrem** _____ .

14 pts.   2)   Underline the subject forms which have the variant signal zero:

anus	aquila	<u>sīmia</u>	equus	canis
<u>aper</u>	<u>leo</u>	īnfāns	taurus	<u>vīpera</u>
<u>musca</u>	piscis	lupus	<u>rāna</u>	asinus

3) Now describe these new situations:

6 pts.　　a)　Aq · · · · 　p · · · · · 　cap · · .

Aquila piscem capit _____ .

6 pts.　　b)　C · · · · 　s · · · · · 　dīl · · · · .

Canis sīmiam dīligit _____ .

6 pts.　　c)　Ī · · · · · 　e · · · · 　mor · · · .

Īnfāns equum mordet _____ .

4) Write the Basic Sentences:

8 pts.　　a)　L · · · · 　n · · 　m · · · · · 　l · · · · · .

Lupus nōn mordet lupum _____ .

Latin: Level One Test for Unit Five/8

6 pts.   b) **V** · · · · · ·   **n** · · · · · ·   **p** · · · · .

Vēritās numquam perit   .

5) Here are some review Basic Sentences:
8 pts.   a) **H** · · · · · ·   **d** · · · · · ·   **d** · · · · · ·   **D** · · · · .

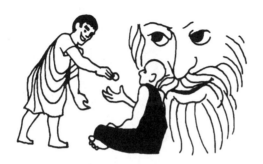

Hilarem datōrem dīligit Deus   .

6 pts.   b) **M** · · · ·   **m** · · · ·   **l** · · · · .

Manus manum lavat   .

8 pts. 6) Pronounce this Basic Sentence:
        Elephantus nōn capit mūrem.

Total
86 pts.

The teacher should listen particularly for aspirated /p/ in **Elephantus,** trilled /r/ in **mūrem,** and short /a/ in **capit.**

NOTE: A table to convert the students' scores to a percentage grade can be found at the end of this book.

4 pts.   1) **Mūrem metuit canis** best describes picture

   __B__ (A/B/C/D).

4 pts.   2) **Aprum canis quaerit** best describes picture

   __C__ (A/B/C/D).

4 pts.   3) Underline the words which can normally fill the adjective slot in the sentence below.

The { walked / <u>happy</u> / was / <u>this</u> / quickly / John / <u>cold</u> } man came into the room.

6 pts.   4) Underline the words which can normally fill the adjective slot in the sentence below.

The man seems { <u>fat.</u> / goes. / gently. / thing. / <u>bright.</u> / <u>stupid.</u> / radio. }

4 pts.   5) In the sentence "The small boy sees the dog" we know that the boy is the one which is small. We know this because of the

   _____**position**_____ of the word "small" in the sentence.

4 pts.   6) Draw a line under the *adjective* in each of these sentences:
   a) <u>Cautus</u> metuit foveam lupus.
   b) Nōn semper aurem <u>facilem</u> habet Fēlīcitās.

2 pts. 7) Underline the word which receives the most emphasis from its *position*.
        Elephantus nōn capit mūrem.

        8) Write these Basic Sentences:
8 pts.   a) **L···· n·· m····· l·····.**

            Lupus nōn mordet lupum _____ .

6 pts.   b) **V······ n······ p·····.**

            Vēritās numquam perit _____ .

6 pts.   c) **V····· v···· r······.**

            Vestis virum reddit _____ .
            Remember to mark the long quantities.

10 pts. 9) Write this Basic Sentence from dictation:

Nōn quaerit aeger medicum ēloquentem

_____

_____ .

2 points per word; 1 point off for wrong macron in questions 9) and 10).

8 pts. 10) Pronounce this Basic Sentence:
Cautus metuit foveam lupus.

Total
66 pts.

Listen particularly for the dipthong /au/ in **cautus**, the separate pronunciation of /u/ and /i/ in **metuit**; and the /w/ sound in **foveam**.

NOTE: A table to convert the students' score to a percentage grade can be found at the end of the book.

1) Write the Basic Sentences. Remember to mark the long quantities.

2 points for each word

12 pts.

a) Et··· c······ ūn·· h···· u····· s···· .

Etiam capillus ūnus habet umbram suam

_____

_____ .

10 pts.

b) N·· qu····· a···· m······ ēl········· .

Nōn quaerit aeger medicum ēloquentem

_____

_____ .

2) Underline just the kernel of the Basic Sentence and label with
- s, - m, - t where appropriate.

         - t   - m   - s

6 pts.

a) **Cautus metuit foveam lupus.**
    - s   - t

4 pts.

b) **Vēritās numquam perit.**

24 pts. 3) Answer these questions on Basic Sentences. Remember that the answer must be in the *same case* as the question word.

4 points for each word; 1 point off for wrong macron.

a) **Quem vestis reddit?**   **Virum**   .

b) **Quis nōn semper**   **aurem facilem?**

        Fēlīcitās

      _____

Latin: Level One Test for Unit Seven/15

c) **Quem lupus nōn mordet?** <u>Lupum</u> .

d) **Quem nōn capit elephantus?** <u>Mūrem</u> .

e) **Quem Deus dīligit?** <u>Hilarem datōrem</u> .

(Two-word answer required)

4) Write these Basic Sentences:

6 pts. a) **V - - - - -   v - - - -   r - - - - - .**

Vestis virum reddit _____ .

12 pts. b) **N - -   s - - - - -   aur - -   f - - - - - -   h - - - -
F - - - - - - - - .**

Nōn semper aurem facilem habet Fēlīcitās _____

_____ .

6 pts. c) **V - - - - - - - -   d - - -   ap - - - - .**

Vēritātem diēs aperit _____ .

Total
80 pts.

1) Write these new Basic Sentences, remembering to put in all the macrons:

Except for question 5), 2 points off for each word; 1 point off for wrong macron.

14 pts.

a) L·· v···· īr····, īr···· l···· n·· v·····.

To facilitate grading, beginning with this Unit only that part of the answer which requires a change is given. When words are repeated without change, they will be represented by dashes whenever feasible.

Lēx videt īrātum, īrātus lēgem nōn videt

_____.

14 pts.

b) V····· v··· fr·····, l···· ag···, f····· l······.

Vulpēs vult fraudem, lupus agnum, fēmina laudem

_____.

10 pts.

c) D··· n·· pr····, d··· n······.

Diem nox premit, diēs noctem

_____.

d) P······ n·· s····· av·······
s·· ir·····.

Pecūnia nōn satiat avāritiam sed irrītat _____

_____ .

2) Answer these questions on the new Basic Sentences. Remember to give the answer in the proper case.

4 pts. a) **Quem fūr cognōscit?** ___**Fūrem**___ .

4 pts. b) **Quis lupum cognōscit?** ___**Lupus**___ .

4 pts. c) **Quis vītam nōn regit?** ___**Sapientia**___ .

3) Expand the sentences with the missing elements to make both kernels complete, as in the sample below.

Sample: **Piscem piscis cognōscit et rāna rānam.** ⟶
Piscem piscis cognōscit et rāna rānam cognōscit.

2 pts. a) **Taurum lupus metuit, lupum taurus.** ⟶

Taurum lupus metuit, lupum taurus

___**metuit**___ .

4 pts. b) **Canis sīmiam nōn metuit sed dīligit.** ⟶

Canis sīmiam nōn metuit sed ___**canis**___

___**sīmiam**___ **dīligit.**

4 pts. c) **Pecūniam quaerit fūr, nōn aeger.** ⟶

Pecūniam quaerit fūr, nōn ___**pecūniam**___

___**quaerit**___ **aeger.**

Latin: Level One Test for Unit Eight/18

4) Write the review Basic Sentences:

12 pts.

a) Et··· c······· ū··· h···· um····
s····.

Etiam capillus ūnus habet umbram suam

_____

_____.

10 pts.

b) N·· qu····· ae··· m······ ēl········

Nōn quaerit aeger medicum ēloquentem

_____

_____.

12 pts.

c) N·· s····· au··· f······ h····
F········.

Nōn semper aurem facilem habet Fēlīcitās

_____

_____.

5) Ask the question which calls for the underlined word in these review Basic Sentences.

4 pts. a) **Vestis virum reddit.**

Quem · · · · · · · · · · · · _____ **?**

4 pts. b) **Crūdēlem medicum intemperāns aeger facit.**

Quis · · · · · · · · · · · · · · · · · · · · _____ **?**

4 pts. c) **Elephantus nōn capit mūrem.**

Quem · · · · · · · · · · · · · · · · · · _____ **?**

Total
118 pts.

TEST FOR UNIT 9 OF *LATIN: LEVEL ONE*

1) Choose your answer from these words, putting it in the same case as the question word: **juvenis, taurus, fēmina, īnfāns, mūs, canis, vulpēs, leō, equus.** Remember the macrons.

2 pts.   a) **Cum quō currit taurus?**

          Cum   juvene   .

2 pts.   b) **Cum quō fēmina est?**

          Cum   īnfante   .

2 pts.   c) **Cum quō mūs est?**

          Cum   cane   .

2 pts.   d)   **Cum quō vulpēs est?**

          Cum _____ **leōne** _____ .

2 pts.   e)   **Cum quō equus est?**

          Cum _____ **taurō** _____ .

     2)   Complete the paradigms:

nominative:	a) **rāna**	b) **Deus**	c) **fraus**

6 pts.   accusative: **rānam**   **Deum**   **fraudem**

6 pts.   ablative: **rānā**   **Deō**   **fraude**

10 pts.   3)   Write the new Basic Sentence.

         N· · · ·   av · · · · · ·   s · · ·   p · · · ·   · · · · .

Nūlla avāritia sine poenā est _____ .

4) And, as usual, there is a Basic Sentence review.

2 points off for each word; 1 off for wrong macron.

14 pts.

a) L·· v···· īr····, īr···· l····
   n·· v····.

Lēx videt īrātum, īrātus lēgem nōn videt
_____

_____.

10 pts.

b) F···· f·· c········ et l···· l····.

Fūrem fūr cognōscit et lupum lupus
_____

_____.

14 pts.

c) V····· v··· fr·····, l···· ag···,
   f····· l·····.

Vulpēs vult fraudem, lupus agnum, fēmina laudem
_____

_____.

Latin: Level One Test for Unit Nine/23

10 pts. d) **V**···· **r**···· **F**······, **n**·· **S**········.

Vītam regit Fortūna, nōn Sapientia

Total
80 pts.

1) Answer the questions by writing out the whole words. Remember macrons and proper case.

2 points off for each word, except for question 2), where each word counts for 1 point, and for question 4), where each word counts 4 points; 1 point off for each wrong macron.

4 pts.   a) **Quō locō taurus est?**
          I - l - - - .

          <u>In</u>   <u>lacū</u> .

4 pts.   b) **Sub quō locō est canis?**
          S - - gr - - - .

          <u>Sub</u>   <u>gradū</u> .

4 pts.   c) **Cum quō est fēmina?**
          C - - ef - - - - - .

          <u>Cum</u>   <u>effigiē</u> .

2) Write the accusative and ablative of the following nouns:

1 point each word for a total of 20 points.

	a) **musca**	b) **asinus**	c) **laus**
3 pts.	**muscam**	asinum	laudem
3 pts.	**muscā**	asinō	laude

	d) quercus	e) faciēs	f) **umbra**
3 pts.	quercum	faciem	umbram
3 pts.	quercū	faciē	umbrā

	g) **saccus**	h) **vulpēs**	i) **anus**
3 pts.	saccum	vulpem	anum
3 pts.	saccō	vulpe	anū

	j) **aciēs**
1 pt.	**aciem**
1 pt.	**aciē**

3) Write the accusative and ablative of the following adjectives:

	a) **hilaris**	b) **cautus**	c) **parva**
6 pts.	hilarem	cautum	parvam
6 pts.	hilarī	cautō	parvā

	d) **intemperāns**
2 pts.	intemperantem
2 pts.	intemperantī

4) Answer these questions on the new Basic Sentences:

4 pts.   a) **"Quō parva vīpera spatiōsum taurum necat?"**

       " Morsū ."

8 pts.   b) **"Sub quō est līs?"**

       " Sub jūdice ."

These questions are more taxing; the students have to know not only the Basic Sentences but the forms used in them. There is no cluing.

Latin: Level One Test for Unit Ten/26

5) Write these Basic Sentences:

10 pts.   a)   **Cr**······   **m**······   **in**·········
             aeg··   **f**·····.

Crūdēlem medicum intemperāns aeger facit _____

_____ .

10 pts.   b)   **D**···   **n**··   **pr**·····,   **d**···   **n**······.

Diem nox premit, diēs noctem _____

_____ .

12 pts.   c)   **P**······   **n**··   **s**·····   **av**·······
             s··   **ir**······.

Pecūnia nōn satiat avāritiam sed irrītat _____

_____ .

10 pts.   d) N···· av······ s··· p···· ····.

Nūlla avāritia sine poenā est _____

Total
102 pts.   _____ .

1)   Give short answers to the questions on this picture:

2 pts.   a) **Quem īnfāns irrītat?**

        ___Sīmiam___ .

2 pts.   b) **Ā quō īnfāns nōn dīligitur?**

        Ā ___sīmiā___ .

2 pts.   c) **Ā quō sīmia irrītātur?**

        Ab___īnfante___ .

2 pts.   d) **Quem sīmia nōn dīligit?**

        ___Īnfantem___ .

2)   Give short answers to the questions on this picture:

2 pts.   a) **Quem agnus metuit?**

        ___Aquilam___ .

2 pts.   b) **Quem aquila capit?**

        ___Agnum___ .

2 pts.   c) **Ā quō agnus capitur?**

        Ab ___aquilā___ .

2 pts.   d) **Ā quō aquila nōn premitur?**

        Ab ___agnō___ .

3) Write the accusative and ablative of the adjective-noun combinations which follow:

a) **crūdēlis medicus**   b) **canis magnus**

8 pts.   **crūdēlem medicum**   **canem magnum**

8 pts.   **crūdēlī medicō**   **cane magnō**

4 pts. 4) Underline the one word which receives the most emphasis from its position:
Vulpēs vult fraudem, lupus agnum, fēmina laudem.

5) Transform these sentences from active to passive.

6 pts.   a) **Vir fēminam quaerit.** ⟶
Ā · · · · · · · · · · · · · · · itur.

Ā virō fēmina quaeritur   .

6 pts.   b) **Anus juvenem tenet.** ⟶
Ab · · · · · · · · · · · · ētur.

Ab anū juvenis tenētur   .

6 pts.   c) **Piscis vīperam mordet.** ⟶
Ā · · · · · · · · · · · · · · ētur.

Ā pisce vīpera mordētur   .

6) These questions are on a new Basic Sentence:

4 pts.   a) **Quem canis parvus saepe tenet?**   **Aprum**   .

8 pts.   b) **Ā quō aper magnus saepe capitur? Ā cane nōn**

magnō or **Ā cane parvō**   .

7) Answer these questions on familiar Basic Sentences. The answers all require a transformation of the original word. Remember that the answer must be in the same case as the question word and have all the long quantities marked by macrons.

4 pts.   a) **Ā quō spatiōsus taurus morsū necātur?**

Ā   vīperā   .

4 pts.   b) **Ā quō vīta regitur? Ā   Fortūnā**   .

4 pts.   c) **Quis ab elephantō nōn capitur?   Mūs**   .

Total
78 pts.

TEST FOR UNIT 12 OF *LATIN: LEVEL ONE*

1) Write the paradigms of these nouns:

8 pts.

a) **vitium** _____

vitium _____

vitiō _____

b) **opus** _____

opus _____

opere _____

4 pts.

c) **auctor** _____

auctōrem _____

auctōre _____

2) Write the new Basic Sentences illustrated by these pictures:

6 pts.

a) S · · · · · · · · v · · · ob · · · · · · · · · .

Sapientia vīnō obumbrātur _____ .

10 pts.

b) N · · · · · · p · · · · ' · · · s · · ·
p · · · · ' · · v · · · · · · · .

Numquam perīc'lum sine perīc'lō vincitur _____

_____ .

8 pts.   c)   **M··· r····· b··· p········.**

Mēns rēgnum bona possidet _____ .

3)   Answer these questions on the new Basic Sentences:

4 pts.   a) **Sine quō est nēmō?**

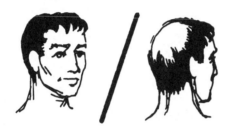

Sine ___vitiō___ .

4 pts.   b) **Quid ab auctōre laudātur?**

___**Opus**___ .

4 pts.   4)   Answer these questions on review Basic Sentences:
         a) **Quid numquam perit?**

___**Vēritās**___ .

Latin: Level One Test for Unit Twelve/32

4 pts.   b)   **Quid fēmina vult?**

<u>**Laudem**</u>   .

4 pts.   c)   **Quālem medicum facit intemperāns aeger?**

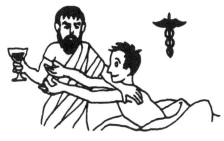

<u>**Crūdēlem**</u>   .

4 pts.   d)   **Quālem aurem nōn semper habet Fēlīcitās?**

<u>**Facilem**</u>   .

8 pts.   e)   **Quid agit parva vīpera?**

<u>**Taurum necat** or **Spatiōsum taurum morsū necat.**</u>
(Two-word answer satisfactory)

Total
68 pts.

1) Answer these questions on the new Basic Sentences:

8 pts.   a) **Ā quō dōnātur et genus et forma?**

Ā ____**Rēgīnā Pecūniā**____ .
(Two-word answer required)

4 pts.   b) **Quid ab īnsānō mediō flūmine quaeritur?**

____**Aqua**____ .

4 pts.   c) **Quālem aquam habet fōns impūrus?**

____**Impūram**____ .
(Is each answer in the same case as its question word?)

2) Give the paradigms of these noun-adjective combinations:

16 pts.   a) **magnum opus**

   magnum opus

   magnō opere

b) **canis magnus**

   canem magnum

   cane magnō

16 pts.   c) **leō parvus**

   leōnem parvum

   leōne parvō

d) **hilare dictum**

   hilare dictum

   hilarī dictō

16 pts.   e) **īrātus fūr**

   īrātum fūrem

   īrātō fūre

f) **crūdēlis spēs**

   crūdēlem spem

   crūdēlī spē

16 pts.   g) **facile genus**

   facile genus

   facilī genere

h) **magnus lacus**

   magnum lacum

   magnō lacū

16 pts.   i) **blanda ōrātiō**

   blandam ōrātiōnem

   blandā ōrātiōne

j) **medium flūmen**

   medium flūmen

   mediō flūmine[1]

[1] It is quite true that the ablative **mediō flūmine** is given in the Basic Sentence in question 1), b) and is required in the paradigm for **medium flūmen**, but experience has shown that only the bright students, who know the forms anyway, will note this coincidence.

3) Give the new Basic Sentences which these pictures illustrate:

10 pts.   a) **M··· s··· ·· c······ s···.**

Mēns sāna in corpore sānō

12 pts. b) **R·· nōn sp··, f····· nōn d·····,
qu····· am····.**

Rem ··· spem, factum ··· dictum,

quaerit amīcus _____

_____

10 pts. c) **H···· s··· v······ bl···· ōr·····.**

Habet suum venēnum blanda ōrātiō _____

_____

8 pts. 4) Give these review Basic Sentences:
a) **S·· j····· l·· ··t.**

Sub jūdice līs est _____

_____

b) Ā c··· nōn m···· s···· t······ a···.

Ā cane ··· magnō saepe tenētur aper _____

_____ .

12 pts. c) L·· v···· īr····, īr···· l···· nōn v····.

Lēx videt īrātum, īrātus lēgem ··· videt _____

_____ .

Total
158 pts.

1) Complete the description of the following pictures:

6 pts. a) **Jūd · · cum fēm · · · · lītem ha · · · ·.**

Jūdex · · · fēminīs · · · · · habet _____

_____ .

6 pts. b) **Vīn · · ā sīm · · · b · · ·tur.**

Vīnum · sīmiīs bibitur _____ .

2) Answer the questions on these pictures:

4 pts. a) **Quī aquam bibunt?**

Asinī _____ .

4 pts.   b)   **Quōs metuit fēmina?**

      Sīmiās .

4 pts.   c)   **Quī ā vulpe inveniuntur?**

      Rānae .

4 pts.   d)   **Quōs mūs irrītat?**

      Elephantōs .

3)   Write the paradigms of these nouns:

20 pts.   a) **rāna**   **rānae**   b) **taurus**   **taurī**

        rānam   **rānās**   **taurum**   **taurōs**

        rānā   **rānīs**   **taurō**   **taurīs**

10 pts.   c) **aper**   **aprī**

        aprum   **aprōs**

        aprō   **aprīs**

Latin: Level One Test for Unit Fourteen/40

10 pts. 4) Write the new Basic Sentence illustrated by this picture:

M··· ·· c······· f······ v······ v·····.

Malō in cōnsiliō fēminae vincunt virōs _____

_____ .

5) Answer these questions on the new Basic Sentences:

4 pts. a) **Quō dī coluntur?**

_____ **Religiōne** _____ .

4 pts. b) **Ā quō muscae nōn capiuntur?**

Ab _____ **aquilā** _____ .

4 pts. c) **Quem lacrimae pāscunt?**

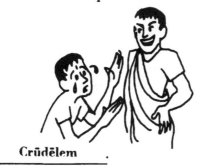

_____ **Crūdēlem** _____ .

6) Write the following review Basic Sentences:

10 pts.   a)   **D··· n·· pr····, d··· n·····.**

Diem nox premit, diēs noctem _____

_____ .

6 pts.   b)   **S········ v··· ob········.**

Sapientia vīnō obumbrātur _____

_____ .

10 pts.   c)   **Īn···· m···· fl···· qu····· aqu··.**

Īnsānus mediō flūmine quaerit aquam _____

_____ .

10 pts.   d) **H····· s··· v······ bl···· ōr·····.**

Habet suum venēnum blanda ōrātiō _____

_____ .

Total
116 pts.

1) Answer these questions on the following pictures:

4 pts. a) **Quem anūs cūrant? Aegrum** or **virum, juvenem,**

medicum, etc. _____ .

4 pts. b) **Ā quibus aeger cūrātur?   Ab** _____ **anibus** _____ .

4 pts. c) **Quōs sīmia pāscit?** _____ **Īnfantēs** _____ .

4 pts. d) **Ā quō īnfantēs pāscuntur?   Ā** _____ **sīmiā** _____ .

4 pts. e) **Quid fūrēs tenent?** _____ **Saccum** _____ .

4 pts. f) **Ā quibus saccus tenētur?   Ā** _____ **fūribus** _____ .

2) Fill in the missing blanks in order to describe these pictures:

4 pts.   a) Īnf····· sīm··· pāscunt.

Īnfantēs sīmiam ·······_____ .

Do not accept **Īnfāns sīmiam pāscunt** since the verb shows that the subject is plural.

4 pts.   b) T···· sub qu·······s stant.

Taurī ··· quercibus ·····_____ .

The cluing shows that the answer is **quercibus** and not **quercū**.

4 pts.   c) Juv···· stultus arc·· suōs lavat.

Juvenis ······· arcūs ···· ·····
_____
_____ .

Latin: Level One Test for Unit Fifteen/46

3) Decline in the singular and the plural.

20 pts.   a) **fovea**   **foveae**   b) **agnus**   **agnī**

          foveam   **foveās**   **agnum**   **agnōs**

          foveā   **foveīs**   **agnō**   **agnīs**

20 pts.   c) **auctor**   **auctōrēs**   d) **saltus**   **saltūs**

          auctōrem **auctōrēs**   **saltum**   **saltūs**

          auctōre   **auctōribus**   **saltū**   **saltibus**

10 pts.   e) **rēs**   **rēs**

          rem   **rēs**

          rē   **rēbus**

6 pts.   4) In Latin we tell which noun an adjective modifies by the fact that the adjective is in the same   case ,   number , and   gender   as the noun with which it agrees.

5) Decline the following noun-plus-adjective combinations. Remember, it is possible that the adjective is not in the same declension as the noun.

20 pts.   a) **fōns pūrus**   **fontēs pūrī**

          fontem pūrum   **fontēs pūrōs**

          fonte pūrō   **fontibus pūrīs**

20 pts.   b) **blanda ōrātiō**   **blandae ōrātiōnēs**

          blandam ōrātiōnem **blandās ōrātiōnēs**

          blandā ōrātiōne   **blandīs ōrātiōnibus**

6 pts.   6) Underline the nouns in this list which are *nominative* case:
imitātiō, taurō, nēmō, ōrātiō,
equō, saccō, lupō, vitiō

4 pts.   7) Underline the nouns in this list which are *nominative* case:
muscās, foveās, vēritās,
poenās, lacrimās, fēlīcitās

8) Write the new Basic Sentences which these pictures illustrate:

12 pts.   a) P···· D···, n·· pl····, asp···· m····.

Pūrās Deus, nōn plēnās, aspicit manūs _____

_____ .

8 pts.   b) ·· au····· c··········· as····· .

Ex auribus cognōscitur asinus _____ .

9) Answer the questions on these new Basic Sentences:
   Stultī timent Fortūnam, sapientēs ferunt.

Only 2 points each because the words
are found in the Basic Sentences.

2 pts.   a) **Ā quibus Fortūna timētur?**   ___Ā stultīs___ .

Fortūna fortēs metuit, īgnāvōs premit.

2 pts.   b) **Quī ā Fortūnā premuntur?**   ___Īgnāvī___ .

10) Write the review Basic Sentences which these pictures illustrate:

10 pts.   a) M··· s··· ·· c······ s··· .

Mēns sāna in corpore sānō _____ .

8 pts.   b) **C····· m····· f····· l····.**

Cautus metuit foveam lupus _____

_____.

10 pts.   c) **Cr······ l······· p·······,**
                n·· fr········.

Crūdēlis lacrimīs pāscitur, nōn frangitur _____

_____.

8 pts.   d) **N··· s··· v···· ····.**

Nēmō sine vitiō est _____.

Total
202 pts.

1) Write the paradigms of the following nouns; be sure to observe which are neuter.

20 pts.

a) **rēgnum** **rēgna**   b) **genus** **genera**

   rēgnum **rēgna**   **genus** **genera**

   rēgnō **rēgnīs**   **genere** **generibus**

20 pts.

c) **capillus** **capillī**   d) **mūs** **mūrēs**

   capillum **capillōs**   **mūrem** **mūrēs**

   capillō **capillīs**   **mūre** **mūribus**

8 pts. 2) Change the underlined words from singular to plural.

a) **Sine factō: Sine**   **factīs** .

b) **Ex opere: Ex** **operibus** .

c) **Vir vitium habet: Vir** **vitia** **habet.**

d) **Flūmen ab īnsānō quaeritur:**

    Flūmina **ab īnsānō quaeruntur.**

6 pts. 3) Underline the words which are the ambiguous nominative-accusative plural neuter:
Fortūna Fāta rēgīna aqua respōnsa rēgna vīta

10 pts. 4) Write the new Basic Sentences which these pictures illustrate:
a) **M- - - - -- c- - - - -, p- - - - n- - - - - - - -.**

Magna dī cūrant, parva neglegunt

8 pts.   b)   P···· l···· c······ an····.

Parva levēs capiunt animōs _____

_____ .

5)   Answer these questions on the new Basic Sentences:

4 pts.   a)   **Ā quibus nōlēns trahitur, volēns dūcitur?**

Ā _____ **Fātīs** _____ .

4 pts.   b)   **Quem Fāta trahunt?**

_____ **Nōlentem** _____ .

4 pts.   c)   **Quālibus lēgibus regunt Fāta orbem?**

_____ **Certīs (lēgibus)** _____ .

4 pts.   d)   **Quālēs lēgēs habent Fāta, certās an incertās?**

_____ **Certās** _____ .

6) Answer these questions on review Basic Sentences:
   Vestis virum reddit.

4 pts.   a) **Ex quō cognōscitur vir? Ex** _____veste_____ .

Parva necat morsū spatiōsum vīpera taurum.

4 pts.   b) **Quae animālia vīperās parvās saepe metuunt?**

_____**Taurī**_____

Auctor opus laudat.

4 pts.   c) **Ā quibus sua opera laudantur?**

Ab _____**auctōribus**_____ .

Ex auribus cognōscitur asinus.

4 pts.   d) **Quae membra possidet asinus stultus?**

_____**Aurēs** or **Aurēs longās**_____ .

Religiō deōs colit, superstitiō violat.

4 pts.   e) **Ā quibus religiō laudātur? Ā** _____**dīs** or **deīs**_____ .
Total
108 pts.

EXTRA READINGS*
Here are some sentences which you have never seen before. Explain
what they mean. You will notice that in the first sentence *every word
is unknown*. But this is not an impossible problem. Every word has
an English derivative. Underlined words are those which have not
yet appeared in *Latin: Level One*.

                     - t   - s   - m   - s   - m
17 pts.   a) **Vertit lympha rotam, rota petram,**
                     - s   - m
           petra farīnam. Med.

           Water turns the wheel, the wheel turns the (mill) stone,

           and the stone (turns) grinds the flour[1]

           _____ .

                     - s   - m   - t
9 pts.   b) **Līs lītem generat.** Anon.

           One lawsuit creates another[2]

           _____ .

The translations for a), b), c) are
only suggestions; many others are
possible. The student may indicate
the structure either by labelling the
parts of the kernel as indicated or
by metaphrasing: The **lympha vertit** s
the **rotam,** etc.

[1]Our activities are all part of a larger
plan.

[2]If you sue someone, you may find
yourself sued in turn.

13 pts.

prepositional modifier   - **s**   - **t**

c) **(Sub omnī lapide) scorpiō dormit.** Anon.

Under every stone sleeps a scorpion[3]

_____ .

Total
39 pts.

[3]Danger lurks everywhere.

*It is suggested that the score on the Unit and the score on the sight passages be recorded separately. As explained in the "Introduction to Testing," there will be wide variation of ability to read these sentences. For ways to assist the student, the teacher may read "Testing of Sight Readings" in the "Introduction to Testing."

Although numbers are given after each sentence and the amounts totaled in the tests in the "Extra Readings" for this Unit and the succeeding Units, these numbers are only to indicate the proportion of weight which each sentence should carry in the teacher's judgment of the students' work. For example, almost perfect performance on sentence "a)" would count almost twice as much as perfect performance on sentence "b)", etc. Perhaps the sentences can be scored by letter grade: "A" for almost perfect performance, "B" for good, "C" for fair, etc. In the final analysis, the teacher must decide in view of the experience and capacity of the students what constitutes satisfactory performance.

1) Answer these new questions on pictures which occurred in this Unit.

4 pts.   a) **Quid hī fortēs ducēs regunt?**

_____Aciem_____ .

A personal noun like **virōs** is also acceptable since the impersonal noun **aciēs** is a collective noun for persons such as men.

4 pts.   b) **Quod animal juvenis in manibus tenet?**

_____Mūrem_____ .

4 pts.   c) **Ā quibus animālibus aqua bibitur?**

Ab _____elephantīs_____ .

2) Write the paradigms of the following words. Notice that you are told to what declension each word belongs.

	1st			2d	
20 pts. a)	īra	īrae	b)	animus	animī
	īram	īrās		animum	animōs
	īrā	īrīs		animō	animīs

2d neuter			3d	
c) vitium	vitia	**d) īnfāns**	īnfantēs	

20 pts.

2d neuter		3d	
vitium	vitia	**īnfāns**	īnfantēs
vitium	vitia	īnfantem	īnfantēs
vitiō	vitiīs	īnfante	īnfantibus

3d neuter		5th	
e) genus	genera	**f) diēs**	diēs
genus	genera	diem	diēs
genere	generibus	diē	diēbus

20 pts.

6 pts. 3) This will show whether you know how to figure out the meaning of new Latin words from their stems and suffixes, or from their English derivatives. Choose the word to complete the sentences from this list:

āctiō, rēs, virtūs, locus
animal, vitium, membrum, homō

a) **"Quid est neglegentia?" "** ____Vitium____ **est."**

Variant answers are possible; could also be **āctiō**.

b) **"Quid est Forum Rōmānum?" "** ____Locus____ **est."**

c) **"Quid est gladiātor?" "** ____Homō____ **est."**

4) Write the new Basic Sentences which these pictures illustrate:

6 pts. a) **V · · · v · · · · · · t.**

____Vīta vīnum est____.

8 pts. b) **F · · · · b · · · · fr · · · · · · · t.**

____Forma bonum fragile est____.

Latin: Level One Test for Unit Seventeen/56

5) Answer these new questions on the new Basic Sentences:

4 pts. a) **Quibus membrīs juvenēs amantēs dūcuntur?**

_____**Oculīs**____ .

6 pts. b) **Quālibus cōnsiliīs regit Deus orbem?**

Cōnsiliīs jūstīs____ , **fortibus**____ , **patientibus**____ .

Only 2 points each since the answers are easily suggested by the Basic Sentence.

4 pts. c) **Quantam vītam habet homō?**

_____**Brevem** or **Brevem vītam**_____ .

2 points each word for the alternate answer.

6) Answer these questions on Review Basic Sentences. Remember, the answer *must* be in the same case as the question word.
Pūrās Deus, nōn plēnās, aspicit manūs.

4 pts. a) **Quālibus manibus Deus colitur?**

Manibus____**pūrīs**____ .

Latin: Level One Test for Unit Seventeen/57

Lupus nōn mordet lupum.

4 pts.   b) **Quae animālia lupī dīligunt?**   <u>   **Lupōs**   </u> .

Crūdēlem medicum intemperāns aeger facit.

8 pts.   c) **Quī ab intemperantibus aegrīs saepe irrītantur?**

<u>   **Blandī medicī**   </u> .

(Two-word answer required)

Total
122 pts.

Any other reasonable adjective acceptable.

EXTRA READINGS

Underlined words are those which have not yet appeared in *Latin: Level One*. Explain the meaning of the following new sentences:

       - m   - t   - s   - s   - m

13 pts.   a) **Fāmam cūrant multī, paucī <u>cōnscientiam</u>.** Pseudo-Publilius Syrus

<u>Many people are concerned for their reputation, but few</u>

<u>for their conscience[1]</u>

_____ .

       - m   - s   - t

11 pts.   b) **Deōs nēmō <u>sānus</u> timet.** Seneca, *Dē Ben.* 4.19.1

<u>No sane person fears the gods[2]</u>

_____ .

Total
24 pts.

[1]Most people are satisfied with appearing to be honest.

[2]No stable person is superstitious and fearful of the gods.

1) Answer each question. Remember that the answer must be in the same case as the question word.

I   II

III   IV

4 pts.   a) **"Quotō in orbe est canis currēns?"**

        " **Tertiō** in orbe."

4 pts.   b) **Quotō in orbe est fūr?"**

        " **Quārtō** in orbe."

4 pts.   c) **Quotō in orbe est leō?"**

        " **Prīmō** in orbe."

4 pts.   d) **Quotō in orbe est medicus?"**

        " **Secundō** in orbe."

2) Write the paradigms of the following nouns:

	1st			2d	
20 pts. a)	**rāna**	**rānae**	b)	**taurus**	**taurī**
	rānam	**rānās**		**taurum**	**taurōs**
	rānā	**rānīs**		**taurō**	**taurīs**

	2d neuter			3d	
20 pts.	c) **rēgnum**	**rēgna**	d) **mūs**	**mūrēs**
	rēgnum	**rēgna**		**mūrem**	**mūrēs**
	rēgnō	**rēgnīs**		**mūre**	**mūribus**

	3d neuter			4th	
20 pts.	e) **flūmen**	**flūmina**	f) **quercus**	**quercūs**
	flūmen	**flūmina**		**quercum**	**quercūs**
	flūmine	**flūminibus**		**quercū**	**quercibus**

	5th	
10 pts.	g) **rēs**	**rēs**
	rem	**rēs**
	rē	**rēbus**

3) Answer these questions on technical terms:

6 pts.   a)   The form **lītigāns** is called a   <u>present participle</u> .

6 pts.   b)   **Inventus** is the past participle of the verb   <u>**invenit**</u> .

6 pts.   c)   The **in-** part of the word **incertus** is called a   <u>prefix</u> .

6 pts.   d)   The **-tās** part of **crūdēlitās** is called a   <u>suffix</u> .

4) Here you can show that you know how to figure out the meaning of new Latin words from their stem and suffix.

4 pts.   a)   **"Estne 'crūdēlitās' vitium an homō?"**

     "   <u>**Vitium**</u> ."

4 pts.   b)   **"Estne 'amātor' āctiō an homō?"**

     "   <u>**Homō**</u> ."

4 pts.   c)   **"Estne 'jūstitia' virtūs an locus?"**

     "   <u>**Virtūs**</u> ."

Latin: Level One Test for Unit Eighteen/60

5) Write the new Basic Sentences which these pictures illustrate.

12 pts.   a) .. v...... p..... ..t v... f........ .

In virtūte posita est vēra fēlīcitās
_____

_____ .

24 pts.   b) Thāis h.... n....., n..... Laecānia
               d.....,
               Qu.. r.... e..? Ēm.... h... h....,
               i... s... .

..... habet nigrōs, niveōs .... dentēs,

Quae ratiō est? Ēmptōs haec habet, illa suōs
_____

_____ .

10 pts. 6) Write the review Basic Sentences which these pictures illustrate:
            a) N...... p....'... s... p....'..
                v........ .

Numquam perīc'lum sine perīc'lō vincitur
_____

_____ .

Latin: Level One Test for Unit Eighteen/61

8 pts.   b)   **Cr····· r·· a··· ···.**

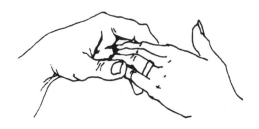

Crēdula rēs amor est _____

_____ .

12 pts.   c)   **Et g···· ·· f····· R····· P······ d·····.**

Et genus et formam Rēgīna Pecūnia dōnat _____

_____ .

Total
188 pts.

EXTRA READINGS
Underlined words are those which have not yet appeared in *Latin: Level One.*

7)   Explain the meaning of the following new sentences:

      · m   · t   · s

9 pts.   a)   **Mulierem ōrnat silentium.** Translation of Sophocles

Silence becomes a woman[1] _____ .   [1]Men don't like women who talk too
      · s   · m   · t   much.

9 pts.   b)   **Rēs amīcōs invenit.** Anon.

Money finds friends[2] _____ .   [2]If you are rich, you will have a lot
Total   of false friends.
18 pts.

TEST FOR UNIT 19 OF *LATIN: LEVEL ONE*

1) Construct the paradigm of these nouns which you have never seen. Notice that you are given two of the six forms and that you are also told to what declension each noun belongs.

	1st			2d	
16 pts.	a) **patria**	**patriae**	b)	**dominus**	**dominī**
	patriam	**patriās**		**dominum**	**dominōs**
	patriā	**patriīs**		**dominō**	**dominīs**

	2d neuter			3d	
16 pts.	c) **exemplum**	**exempla**	d)	**rēx**	**rēgēs**
	exemplum	**exempla**		**rēgem**	**rēgēs**
	exemplō	**exemplīs**		**rēge**	**rēgibus**

	3d neuter			4th	
16 pts.	e) **tempus**	**tempora**	f)	**vultus**	**vultūs**
	tempus	**tempora**		**vultum**	**vultūs**
	tempore	**temporibus**		**vultū**	**vultibus**

	5th	
2 pts.	g) **fidēs** (no plural)	
	fidem	
	fidē	

2) Underline the verb or verbs which will fit into the pattern:

4 pts.   a) **Muscās leōnēs nōn**   {
premunt.
capiuntur.
sunt.
currunt.

4 pts.   b) **Vir orbēs**   {
vident.
scrībuntur.
indicat.
laudant.

8 pts.   c) **Leōnēs animālia** $\begin{cases} \text{necant.} \\ \overline{\text{sunt.}} \\ \overline{\text{metuit.}} \\ \text{dīliguntur.} \end{cases}$

3) Answer these questions, using the new adverb forms:

4 pts.   a) **"Quāliter virī hilarēs cēnant?"**

                    "   <u>Hilariter   </u>."

4 pts.   b) **Quāliter medicus cautus aegrum cūrat?"**

                    " <u>Cautē   </u>."

4 pts.   c) **"Quāliter Deus jūstus orbem regit?"**

                    "   <u>Jūstē   </u>."

4) Give an English translation of these sentences which contain relative clauses. Be careful with the relative pronouns which are in the accusative case.

12 pts.   a) **Aprum, quem canis tenet, vir metuit.** =

                    <u>The man fears the boar which the dog is holding</u>

                    _____.

14 pts.   b) **Fortūna, ā quā fortēs adjuvantur, īgnāvōs neglegit.** =

                    <u>Fortune, by whom brave men are helped, neglects (ignores)</u>

                    <u>cowardly people</u>

                    _____.

12 pts.   c) **Intemperantia, quae aegrum laedit, vitium est.** =

                    <u>Intemperance. which harms a sick person, is a fault</u>

                    _____.

5) Make one sentence out of each pair by substituting the right form of the relative pronoun for the underlined word:

Count 4 points for relative pronoun and 1 point for every other word.

9 pts.   a) **Mulier bella est; mulier laudem vult.**
                    M · · · · ·,   qu · · <u>l · · · · ·</u> v · · ·,   b · · · · · · t.

                    <u>Mulier, quae laudem vult, bella est</u>

                    _____.

Latin: Level One Test for Unit Nineteen/64

10 pts.   b)   **Jūdex innocentem absolvit; jūdicem omnēs jūstē laudant.**

**J····,   qu··   om···   j····   l······,
in········   abs······.**

<u>**Jūdex, quem omnēs jūstē laudant, innocentem**</u>

<u>**absolvit**</u>   .

4 pts.   6)   Answer this new question on the new Basic Sentence:
"Quōcum cēnat Caeciliānus?"

   "   **Cum aprō**   ."   Acceptable: **Cum aprō, Cum bellō**
   (Several possible answers; write just one.)   **convīvā, Cum convīvā,** and **Cum**
                                                          amīcō.

18 pts.   7)   Write the new Basic Sentence which this picture illustrates:
**N····   qu··   ··   fl·····   m····   ···   in   m···
p······   ···· .**

<u>**Nāvis quae in flūmine magna est · · mari**</u>

<u>**parvula est**</u>

                                            .

8 pts.   8)   Call these people, using the new calling form:

Mārcus.   <u>**Mārce**</u>   !   **Titus.**   <u>**Tite**</u>   !

     9)   Answer these questions on the following review Basic Sentence:
Īra furor brevis est.

8 pts.   a)   **"Quālis est homō quī īrātus est?"**
"Īns···· ··t."

          <u>**Īnsānus est**</u>

4 pts.   b)   **"Quid est animal quod muscās nōn quaerit?"**

      <u>**Aquila**</u>   .

10) Write the review Basic Sentences which these pictures illustrate:

10 pts. a) **Oc--- s--- -- am--- d----.**

Oculī sunt in amōre ducēs _____

_____ .

10 pts. b) **Ā f---· p--- p--- dē----- a---.**

Ā fonte pūrō pūra dēfluit aqua _____

_____ .

Total
197 pts.

EXTRA READINGS
Underlined words are those which have not yet appeared in *Latin: Level One*. Explain the meaning of the following new sentences:

                    -s   - m   - t
11 pts. a) **Piscēs magnī parvulōs comedunt.** Anon.

Big fish eat little fish[1] _____ . [1]Survival of the fittest.
              - t   - s

15 pts. b) **Nōn convalēscit planta quae saepe trānsfertur.**
Seneca, *Ep.* 2.3

The plant (tree) which is often transplanted does not

flourish[2] _____ . [2]People who move about from one
place to another do not prosper.

Total
26 pts.

Latin: Level One Test for Unit Nineteen/66

1) Answer these questions on these pictures:

4 pts.   a) **"Cui anus similis est?" "** __Anuī__ **."**

4 pts.   b) **"Cui vīta brevis est?" "** __Mūrī__ **."**

4 pts.   c) **"Cui aper pulcher vidētur?" "** __Aprō__ **."**

2) Write just the *singular* paradigm of the following words, includ-
    ing the four cases you now know:

	a) **patria**	b) **beneficium**	c) **mors**
6 pts.	**patriam**	**beneficium**	**mortem**
6 pts.	**patriā**	**beneficiō**	**morte**
6 pts.	**patriae**	**beneficiō**	**mortī**

	d) manus	e) faciēs
4 pts.	manum	faciem
4 pts.	manū	faciē
4 pts.	manuī	faciēī

4 pts.   3) Answer this question on a new Basic Sentence:

"Ā quō asinus laudātur?" "Ab _____asinō_____."

16 pts. 4) Write the new Basic Sentence which this picture illustratcs:
M··· īn····· f····, j····· ac····,
n···· s··· s···.

Mors īnfantī fēlīx, juvenī acerba, nimis sēra senī
_____

_____ .

5) Write the review Basic Sentences which these pictures illustrate:

22 pts. a) Thāis h···· n·····, n····· Laecānia
d······.
Quae r···· ··t? Ēm···· h··· h····,
i··· s··s.

····· habet nigrōs, niveōs ········ dentēs.
_____

···· ratiō est? Ēmptōs haec habet, illa suōs
_____

_____ .

10 pts.　　b)　**M···· d· c·····, p···· n········.**

Magna dī cūrant, parva neglegunt

_____ .

10 pts.　　c)　**In v······ p····· ··t v··· f········.**

·· virtūte posita est vēra fēlīcitās

_____ .

Total
104 pts.

EXTRA READINGS

Underlined words are those which have not yet appeared in *Latin: Level One*. Explain the meaning of the following new sentences:

11 pts.　　a)　**Canis sine dentibus lātrat.** Ennius (quoted by Varro, *Dē Ling. Lat.*)

A dog without teeth barks[1]

_____ .

[1]People who threaten may not be able to carry out their threats.

11 pts.　　b)　**Dōnum forma breve est.** Nemesiānus, *Ecl.* 14.24

Beauty is a short-lived gift[2]

_____ .

[2]We are not young and beautiful very long.

Total
22 pts.

1) Say that these animals are near other animals or near places. Be sure to notice whether the situation calls for singular or plural.

8 pts.   a) **C ---- pr ---- us l -------- -- t.**

Canis proximus leōnibus est

_____ .

8 pts.   b) **T ----- pr ----- s qu ----- -- t.**

Taurus proximus quercuī est

_____ .

8 pts.   c) **M -- pr ----- s ef ------ ---- .**

Mūs proximus effigiēī est

_____ .

2) Write the four cases, singular and plural, of these nouns:

4 pts. a) vīpera   vīperae   b) agnus   agnī

8 pts.   vīperam   vīperās   agnum   agnōs

8 pts.   vīperā   vīperīs   agnō   agnīs

8 pts.   vīperae   vīperīs   agnō   agnīs

4 pts. c) auctor   auctōrēs   d) anus   anūs

8 pts.   auctōrem   auctōrēs   anum   anūs

8 pts.   auctōre   auctōribus   anū   anibus

8 pts.   auctōrī   auctōribus   anuī   anibus

3) Change the underlined ambiguous dative-ablative plural forms to the singular:

2 pts. a) **Nōn cēnat sine aprīs Caeciliānus.** ⟶

        Nōn cēnat sine   aprō   Caeciliānus.

2 pts. b) **Mors juvenibus nōn placet.** ⟶

        Mors   juvenī   nōn placet.

2 pts. c) **Fēmina vīnum aegrīs dat.** ⟶

        Fēmina vīnum   aegrō   dat.

2 pts. d) **Puellae mulieribus serviunt.** ⟶

        Puellae   mulierī   serviunt.

4) Answer these questions on the new Basic Sentences:
   Impōnit fīnem sapiēns et rēbus honestīs.

2 pts. a) **"Quālēs rēs ā sapiente temperanter coluntur?"**

        "Etiam rēs   honestae   ."

   Nēmō līber est quī corporī servit.

2 pts. b) **"Quō regitur quī nimis vīnum bibit?"**

        "   Corpore   suō."

14 pts. 5) Write the Basic Sentence, which this picture describes, about women who marry often.

Mul··· qu·· mul··· nūb·· mul··· n··
pl·····.

Mulier quae multīs nūbit multīs nōn placet

_____ .

6) Answer these questions on review Basic Sentences:
Fāta regunt orbem; certā stant omnia lēge.

2 pts. a) **"Cui imperant Fāta?"**

"   **Orbī**   ."

Religiō deōs colit, superstitiō violat.

2 pts. b) **"Quibus nocet superstitiō?"**

"   **Dīs (Deīs)**   ."

7) Write the review Basic Sentences which these pictures describe:

8 pts. a) **Aqu··· n·· cap·· mus···.**

Aquila nōn capit muscās

_____ .

10 pts.   b)   **Oc · · · s · · · in am · · · duc · ·**

Oculī sunt in amōre ducēs   .

Total
128 pts.

EXTRA READINGS
Underlined words are those which have not yet appeared in *Latin: Level One*.

15 pts.   a)   **Lupus est homō hominī, nōn homō.** Plautus, *Asin.* 495

To his fellow man, a man is a wolf, not a human being[1]   [1]Men sometimes act more like beasts
                                                                  than like men.

                                                                  .

25 pts.   b)   **Gaudēns gaudentī, flēns flentī, pauper egentī, prūdēns prūdentī, stultus placet īnsipientī.** Med.

The happy person pleases one who is happy; one who is sad

finds consolation in another who weeps; the poor man

pleases the needy; the wise person seeks out another wise   [2]Like seeks like.

person; (and) a fool likes a fool[2]   .

Total
40 pts.

1) Answer these questions, similar to those in the Unit:

12 pts. a) "Estne lingua tōta faciēs?"

"M····ē; lingua est p··· f······.

<u>   Minimē; ······ ··· pars faciēī   </u> .

4 pts. b) "Anus rānam adjuvat. Cujus auxiliō ergō rāna adjuvātur?"

"···· auxiliō."

<u> Anūs </u> .

4 pts. c) "Sī fēmina perit, cujus mors est?"

"······· mors est."

<u> Fēminae </u> .

4 pts. d) "Sī taurus vincit, cujus victōria est?"

"····· victōria est."

<u> Taurī </u> .

2) Write the *singular* paradigm (all five cases) of the following nouns:

	a) <u>sīmia</u>	b) <u>exemplum</u>	c) <u>vir</u>
6 pts.	sīmiam	exemplum	virum
6 pts.	sīmiā	exemplō	virō
6 pts.	sīmiae	exemplō	virō
6 pts.	sīmiae	exemplī	virī

	d) <u>canis</u>	e) <u>quercus</u>	f) <u>diēs</u>
6 pts.	canem	quercum	diem
6 pts.	cane	quercū	diē
6 pts.	canī	quercuī	diēī
6 pts.	canis	quercūs	diēī

3) "In hāc sententiā 'Exemplum Deī quisque est in imāgine parvā' cujus cāsūs est nōmen 'exemplum'?"

2 pts. a) " 'Exemplum' est cāsūs <u>   nōminātīvī   </u>."

2 pts. b) " 'Quisque' est cāsūs _____nōminātīvī_____ ."

2 pts. c) " 'Deī' est cāsūs _____genitīvī_____ ."

  4) Questions on new Basic Sentences:

4 pts. a) **"Quō membrō malī servī laeditur dominus?"**

    " _____Linguā_____ ."

4 pts. b) **"Quae animālia morte lupī adjuvantur?"**

    " _____Agnī_____ ."

  5) What Basic Sentence in this Unit expresses approximately this
8 pts. thought?
  Artēs animum hominis faciunt.
  Ōrā · · · cul · · · ani · · · · t.

  Ōrātiō cultus animī est _____ .

  6) Write the new Basic Sentence which this picture illustrates:
8 pts. **Glō · · · umb · · virt · · · · · · t.**

  Glōria umbra virtūtis est _____ .

  7) What review Basic Sentence expresses approximately this
6 pts. thought?
  Juvenēs formā, nōn animō, in amōre dūcuntur.
  Oc · · · sunt in amō · · duc · · ·.

  Oculī · · · · · · amōre ducēs _____ .

  8) Write the review Basic Sentences which these pictures illustrate:
10 pts. a) **Asin · · as · · ·, s · · s · · pul · · · · .**

  Asinus asinō, sūs suī pulcher _____ .

12 pts.   b) **Nē·· līb·· ··t quī corp··· ser····.**

Nēmō līber est quī corporī servit _____

_____ .

16 pts.   c) **R·· nōn sp··, fac··· ··· dic···,
             quae··· amīc··.**

Rem nōn spem, factum nōn dictum, quaerit amīcus _____

_____ .

Total
146 pts.

EXTRA READINGS
Underlined words are those which have not yet appeared in *Latin:
Level One.*

11 pts.   a) **Timor Domínī fōns vītae.** Motto

Fear of God is the spring of life[1] _____

_____ .

13 pts.   b) **Imāgō animī vultus; indicēs oculī.** Cicero, *Dē Or,*
             3.59.221

The face is the mirror of the mind, and the eyes are its

signals[2] _____ .

(·t is missing but must be supplied
in the English version.)

[1]Love and respect for God is the most
essential thing in a person's life.

(·t is missing from each kernel but
must be supplied in the English
sentence, at least with one kernel.)

[2]We can read a person's character in
his face, particularly by looking at
his eyes.

Total
24 pts.

1) Answer the questions on the pictures:

4 pts.   **a)** **"Quōrum aurēs longae sunt?"** "   **Asinōrum**   ."

4 pts.   **b)** **"Quōrum pedēs parvī sunt?"** " **Mūrum** ."

4 pts.   **c)** **"Quōrum dicta acerba sunt?"** " **Anuum** ."

4 pts.   **d)** **"Quōrum vīta brevis est?"** "   **Muscārum**   ."

2) Write the complete paradigm, singular and plural, of the following nouns:

From now on, since the paradigms are largely review, each form will count only one point.

18 pts. a) | puella | puellae | b) | equus | equī |
|---|---|---|---|---|
| puellam | puellās | | equum | equōs |
| puellā | puellīs | | equō | equīs |
| puellae | puellīs | | equō | equīs |
| puellae | puellārum | | equī | equōrum |

18 pts. c) | fātum | Fāta | d) | rēx | rēgēs |
|---|---|---|---|---|
| fātum | Fāta | | rēgem | rēgēs |
| fātō | Fātīs | | rēge | rēgibus |
| fātō | Fātīs | | rēgī | rēgibus |
| fātī | Fātōrum | | rēgis | rēgum |

18 pts. e) | genus | genera | f) | quercus | quercūs |
|---|---|---|---|---|
| genus | genera | | quercum | quercūs |
| genere | generibus | | quercū | quercibus |
| generī | generibus | | quercuī | quercibus |
| generis | generum | | quercūs | quercuum |

9 pts. g) | rēs | rēs |
|---|---|
| rem | rēs |
| rē | rēbus |
| reī | rēbus |
| reī | rērum |

3) Answer these questions on the new Basic Sentences:
Gravis īra rēgum est semper.

4 pts. a) **"Quī, sī īrātī sunt, inopēs laedunt?"**

"   **Rēgēs**   ."

Latin: Level One Test for Unit Twenty-three/80

Rērum hūmānārum domina Fortūna.

4 pts.   b)   **"Ā quō hominēs reguntur?"**

"Ā   Fortūnā   ."

4)   Write the new Basic Sentences which these pictures illustrate:

10 pts.   **Nē · · mort · · · · · omn · · · · hōr · · s · · · t.**

Nēmō mortālium omnibus hōrīs sapit _____

_____ .

12 pts.   **Vī · · mortu · · · · in mem · · · · vīv · · · · e · ·
pos · · · ·.**

Vīta mortuōrum · · memoriā vīvōrum est _____

posita _____

_____ .

4 pts.   5)   Answer this question on a review Basic Sentence:
Plōrātur lacrimīs āmissa pecūnia vērīs.
"Quālēs sunt lacrimae cum pecūnia āmissa est?"

"   Vērae   ."

Latin: Level One Test for Unit Twenty-three/81

6) Write the review Basic Sentences which these pictures illustrate:

22 pts.   N · · cēn · · s · · e ap · · n · · · er, T · · · ,
        Caecili · · · · .
        Bell · · conv · · · · C · · · · · · · · · s hab · · .

Nōn cēnat sine aprō noster, Tite, Caeciliānus.

Bellum convīvam Caeciliānus habet

18 pts.   Nāv · · qu · · · · flū · · · · mag · · · · t in m · · ·
        parv · · · · · t.

Nāvis quae in flūmine magna est · · marī

parvula est

14 pts.   Q · · ping · · flōr · · fl · · · · n · · p · · · · t
        odō · · · · .

Quī pingit flōrem flōris nōn pingit odōrem

Total
167 pts.

EXTRA READINGS

13 pts.　a)　**Patria commūnis est omnium parēns.** Cicero, *Cat.*
　　　　　-s　　　　　　est　　　　　-s
　　　1.7.17

Our country is the common parent of us all[1]

_____ .

13 pts.　b)　**Quī ēbrium lūdificat, laedit absentem.** Anon.
　　　　　　-s　　　　　-t　　-m

He who makes fun of someone who is drunk is harming a

person who is absent[2]

_____ .

Total
26 pts.

Since the students have been having widely different experiences in the Reader it is felt that there is no longer any need to underline words in the Readings which have not yet appeared in **Latin: Level One.** Consequently, this procedure which was initiated in Unit 16 is now being discontinued.

[1] We should all obey and respect our country's laws as we do the wishes of our fathers.

[2] A person who has drunk too much is not in command of himself.

TEST FOR UNIT 24 OF *LATIN: LEVEL ONE*

6 pts.   1)   Write the singular paradigm of **timēre**.

   1st person   **timēo**

   2d person   **timēs**

   3d person   **timet**

8 pts.   2)   Expand with the pronoun which can be the subject of the verb.

   a)   **Tū**   **beneficium dās.**

   b)   **Egō**   **omnibus miserīs noceō.**

   c)   **Tū**   **nōn cēnās sine aprō.**

   d)   **Egō**   **levēs capiō animōs.**

20 pts.   3)   Give the various forms as required: 2 points each word.

   a)   **"Quid est 'difficultās' in cāsū datīvō et**

   numerō singulārī?" "   difficultātī   ."

   b)   **"Quid est 'flōs' in cāsū accūsātīvō et**

   numerō plūrālī?" "   flōrēs   ."

   c)   **"Quid est 'effigiēs' in cāsū genitīvō et**

   numerō singulārī?" "   effigiēī   ."

   d)   **"Quid est 'arcus' in cāsū datīvō et numerō**

   singulārī?" "   arcuī   ."

   e)   **"Quid est 'caelum' in cāsū accūsātīvō et**

   numerō singulārī?" "   caelum   ."

   f)   **"Quid est 'vestis' in cāsū ablātīvō et**

   numerō singulārī?" "   veste   ."

   g)   **"Quid est 'diēs' in cāsū nōminātīvō et**

   numerō plūrālī?" "   diēs   ."

h) **"Quid est 'rāna' in cāsū datīvō et numerō plūrālī?"** " **rānīs** ."

i) **"Quid est 'flūmen' in cāsū genitīvō et numerō plūrālī?"** " **flūminum** ."

j) **"Quid est 'dominus' in cāsū ablātīvō et numerō plūrālī?"** " **dominīs** ."

4) Answer these questions on new Basic Sentences:
Omnia mors poscit; lēx est, nōn poena, perīre.

4 pts.

a) **"Quāliter omnēs pereunt?"**
"**J** · · · · ."

" **Jūstē** ."

Elicits a word which is not in the original sentence and is, therefore, a "comprehension question."

Nātūram quidem mūtāre difficile est.

4 pts.

b) **"Quantōs saltūs nōn facit nātūra?"**

" **magnōs** ."

While strictly speaking, though **quantōs** asks for an adjective of size, and adjectives of quality are elicited by **quālis**, an answer such as **difficilēs** would be acceptable.

12 pts. 5) Write the new Basic Sentence which expresses approximately this thought:
Ille nōn est philosophus vērus, etiam sī aspectū suō philosophō similis est.
Vid · · **bar** · · · **et pal** · · · · ; **philos** · · · · · **nōn** · · · **v** · · · · .

Videō barbam · · **pallium; philosophum**

nōndum videō .

6 pts. 6) Write the new Basic Sentence which this picture illustrates:
Aur · · · · **ten** · · **lup** · · · .

Auribus teneō lupum .

7) Say that it is easy to do these things:

16 pts.

    a) **Vēritātem diēs aperit.** ⟶

       Facil · · ·t v · · · · · · · ap · · · · · .

       Facile est vēritātem aperīre   .

16 pts.

    b) **Auctor opus laudat.** ⟶

       F · · · · · · ·t op · · l · · · · · · .

       Facile est opus laudāre   .

10 pts. 8) Write the review Basic Sentence which expresses approximately this thought:

Sapiēns nihil, etiam in rēbus bonīs, nimis agit.

Imp · · · · f · · · · s · · · · · · et r · · · · h · · · · · · · · .

Impōnit fīnem sapiēns · · rēbus honestīs

                                       .

9) Write the review Basic Sentences which these pictures illustrate:

8 pts.

    a) **Glō · · · um · · · virt · · · · · ·t.**

    Glōria umbra virtūtis est

                                       .

6 pts.

    b) **Vī · · vīn · · · ·t.**

    Vīta vīnum est

                                       .

8 pts.   c)   **For ·· bo ··· frag ··· ·· t.**

Forma bonum fragile est _____

_____ .

Total
124 pts.

EXTRA READINGS

15 pts.   a)   **Multōs timēre dēbet quem multī timent.** Publilius
Syrus

The person whom many people fear ought himself to fear   [1]If people are afraid of you, they may
_____   try to harm you.

many[1]   .

15 pts.   b)   **Saepe creat mollēs aspera spīna rosās.** Med.

The sharp thorn often creates soft roses[2]   _____   [2]Mean fathers often have lovely
daughters.

_____ .

Total
30 pts.

1) Write the paradigms of the following verbs:

    a)   **stāre**   b)   **vidēre**

8 pts.	**stō**	**stāmus**	**videō**	**vidēmus**
8 pts.	**stās**	**stātis**	**vidēs**	**vidētis**
8 pts.	**stat**	**stant**	**videt**	**vident**

    c)   **petere**   d)   **aspicere (-iō)**

8 pts.	**petō**	**petimus**	**aspiciō**	**aspicimus**
8 pts.	**petis**	**petitis**	**aspicis**	**aspicitis**
8 pts.	**petit**	**petunt**	**aspicit**	**aspiciunt**

    e)   **custōdīre**

4 pts.	**custōdiō**	**custōdīmus**
4 pts.	**custōdīs**	**custōdītis**
4 pts.	**custōdit**	**custōdiunt**

Students did not need to be told that these were paradigms of the #2 (present) tense since this is the only tense they know thus far.

10 pts. 2) a) **"Quid est 'necessitās' in cāsū datīvō et numerō singulārī?" "** _____**necessitātī**_____**."**

2 points each word.

    b) **"Quid est 'dolor' in cāsū genitīvō et numerī plūrālī?" "** ___**dolōrum**___**."**

    c) **"Quid est 'poena' in cāsū accūsātīvō et numerō singulārī?" "** ___**poenam**___**."**

    d) **"Quid est 'nōmen' in cāsū accūsātīvō et numerō singulārī?" "** ___**nōmen**___**."**

    e) **"Quid est 'vōx' in cāsū genitīvō et numerō plūrālī?" "** ___**vōcum**___**."**

3 pts. 3) a) Call **Caeciliānus**, using the special calling

form: "_____**Caeciliāne**_____."

3 pts.   b) Call **Sabidius,** using the special calling

form: "____**Sabidī**____."

4 pts. 4) Answer this question on a new Basic Sentence:
"Capere cōnsilium potes; quantus est dolor tuus?"

"_____**Levis (nōn magnus)**_____."   Could also be **parvus;** see note on test for Unit 24, item 4), b).

10 pts. 5) Write the new Basic Sentence which this picture illustrates:
Hōr·· n·· num···, n··ī serē····.

Hōrās nōn numerō, nisī serēnās _____

_____.

4 pts. 6) Answer this question on a review Basic Sentence:
Nēmō mortālium omnibus hōrīs sapit.
"Quid tū nōn semper agis?"

"Egō nōn semper____sapiō____."

10 pts. 7) Write the review Basic Sentences which these pictures illustrate:
a) **M··ō in c·······ō fēm···· vinc··· vir···.**

Malō ·· cōnsiliō fēminae vincunt virōs _____

_____.

16 pts.   b)   **M · · s īnf · · · · fēl · ·, juv · · · acer · ·,
              n · · · s sēr · sen · .**

Mors īnfantī fēlīx, juvenī acerba, nimis sēra senī

_____.

8 pts.   c)   **Mo · · lu · · agn · · vī · · .**

Mors lupī agnīs vīta _____.

Total
128 pts.

EXTRA READINGS

11 pts.   a)   **Praeterita mūtāre nōn possumus.** Anon.

              We cannot change the past[1] _____   [1]Regret is foolish.

              _____.

13 pts.   b)   **Effugere cupiditātem rēgnum est vincere.** Publilius
              Syrus

              To escape desire is to win a throne[2] _____   [2]The true philosopher, who is free
                                                                      from foolish desires, is as powerful
              _____.   as a king.

Total
24 pts.

12 pts. 1) a) Write the #1 forms of **cēnāre**:

cēnābam	**cēnābāmus**
cēnābās	**cēnābātis**
cēnābat	**cēnābant**

12 pts. b) Write the #2 forms of **regere**:

regō	**regimus**
regis	**regitis**
regit	**regunt**

12 pts. c) Write the #3 forms of **lavāre**:

lavābō	**lavābimus**
lavābis	**lavābitis**
lavābit	**lavābunt**

12 pts. d) Write the #3 forms of **premere**:

premam	**premēmus**
premēs	**premētis**
premet	**prement**

18 pts. 2) Identify by number (#1, #2, or #3) the tense of the following verb forms which you have not seen before.

a) **saliēmus** #3   b) **quiēscētis** #3

c) **effugiet** #3   d) **laudant** #2

e) **plōrābō** #3   f) **timēs** #2

g) **poscō** #2   h) **dēbēmus** #2

i) **sentiēs** #3

12 pts. 3) a) "Quid est 'tempus' in cāsū genitīvō et

numerō singulārī?" "___temporis___."

b) "Quid est 'lingua' in cāsū accūsatīvō et

numerō plūrālī?" "___linguās___."

c) "Quid est 'quercus' in cāsū genitīvō et

numerō plūrālī?" "___quercuum___."

d) "Quid est 'faciēs' in cāsū accūsātīvō et

numerō singulārī?" "___faciem___."

e) "Quid est 'verbum' in cāsū accūsātīvō et

numerō plūrālī?" "___verba___."

f) "Quid est 'equus' in cāsū genitīvō et

numerō singulārī?" "___equī___."

4) Give the synopses (forms #1, #2, and #3) of the following
verbs in the person and number indicated:

6 pts. a) **manēre,** 2d singular (**tū** as subject)

#1 **manēbās**

#2 **manēs**

#3 **manēbis**

6 pts. b) **obumbrāre,** 1st singular (**egō** as subject)

#1 **obumbrābam**

#2 **obumbrō**

#3 **obumbrābō**

6 pts. c) **effugere** (**-iō**), 2d plural (**vōs** as subject)

#1 **effugiēbātis**

#2 **effugitis**

#3 **effugiētis**

6 pts.   d) **custōdīre**, 2d singular (**tū** as subject)

      #1 **custōdiēbās** _____

      #2 **custōdīs** _____

      #3 **custōdiēs** _____

   5) Answer these questions on these new Basic Sentences:

4 pts.   a) **Quid nōbīs omnibus accidet?"**

      " **Mors** ."

8 pts.   b) **Orbem jam tōtum victor Rōmānus habēbat.**
      "Quem metuēbat tōtus orbis terrārum?"

      " **Victōrem** **Rōmānum** ."

10 pts. 6) Write the new Basic Sentence which this picture illustrates:
      S - - qu - - custōd - - - ips - - c - - - - - - s?

Sed quis custōdiet ipsōs custōdēs
_____ ?

4 pts. 7) Answer this question on a review Basic Sentence:
      Nātūram quidem mūtāre difficile est.
      "Quantā difficultāte mūtātur nātūra?"

      " **Magnā** ."

14 pts. 8) Write the review Basic Sentence which the picture illustrates:
Cae·· duc·· quaer···; n·s s··e du·· err·····.

Caecī ducem quaerunt; nōs sine duce errāmus
_____ .

Total
142 pts.

EXTRA READINGS

11 pts.   a) **Crūdēlitātis māter est avāritia.** Quintilian 9.3.89

Greed is the mother of cruelty[1] _____   [1]It is greed which makes people
                                                          cruel.
_____ .

15 pts.   b) **In magnō grandēs capiuntur flūmine piscēs.** Med.

Big fish are caught in a large river[2] _____   [2]If you want an important position,
                                                          go to a large company.
_____ .

Total
26 pts.

8 pts. 1) a) **"Quō locō puella stat?"**
"Tr - - - - - - - - - - ."

flūmen

" _____Trāns_____ _____flūmen_____ ."

8 pts. b) **"Quō locō sunt mūrēs?"**
"In - - - - - - - - - ."

saccus saccus saccus

" _____Inter_____ _____saccōs_____ ."

12 pts. 2) Write the paradigm of the #5 form of **capiō, capere, cēpī, captus**:

_____cēpī_____	_____cēpimus_____
_____cēpistī_____	_____cēpistis_____
_____cēpit_____	_____cēpērunt_____

20 pts. 3) Here are sentences which contain #5 forms of verbs which you have not seen but whose #2 forms you do know. Transform these #5 verbs to the #2 form in the same number and person.

Two points for each word.

Example: **Tū omnia poposcistī. ——→ Tū omnia poscis.**

a) **Canis aprum momordit. ——→**

Canis aprum _____mordet_____ .

b) **Egō vēritātem quaesīvī. ——→**

Egō vēritātem _____quaerō_____ .

c) Tū lupum īrātum aspexistī. ⟶

   Tū lupum īrātum _____aspicis_____ .

d) Hominēs hōrās serēnās numerāvērunt. ⟶

   Hominēs hōrās serēnās _____numerant_____ .

e) Hominī jūstō nocuimus. ⟶

   Hominī jūstō _____nocēmus_____ .

f) Pedem gradibus imposuī. ⟶

   Pedem gradibus _____impōnō_____ .

g) Certās rēs saepe mīsistis. ⟶

   Certās rēs saepe _____mittitis_____ .

h) Agnī lupum timuērunt. ⟶

   Agnī lupum _____timent_____ .

i) Magnās litterās in gradū scrīpsī. ⟶

   Magnās litterās in gradū _____scrībō_____ .

j) Equum ad lacum dūxistī. ⟶

   Equum ad lacum _____dūcis_____ .

4) Write the principal parts of these verbs:

4 pts.   a) eō, _____īre_____ , _____iī_____ .

6 pts.   b) lūdō, _____lūdere_____ , _____lūsī_____ , _____lūsus_____ .

6 pts.   c) edō, _____edere_____ , _____ēdī_____ , _____ēsus_____ .

4 pts.   d) currō, _____currere_____ , _____cucurrī_____ .

6 pts.   e) videō, _____vidēre_____ , _____vīdī_____ , _____vīsus_____ .

5) Give the noun forms asked for:

2 pts.   a) "Quid est 'sīdus' in cāsū ablātīvō et numerō plūrālī?"

   " _____sīderibus_____ ."

2 pts.   b)   **"Quid est 'fidēs' in cāsū datīvō**

                     et numerō singulārī?" "___fideī___."

2 pts.   c)   **"Quid est 'cursus' in cāsū ablātīvō**

                     et numerō singulārī?" "___cursū___."

2 pts.   d)   **"Quid est 'certāmen' in cāsū ablātīvō et**

                     numerō singulārī?" "___certāmine___."

     6)   Write the new Basic Sentences which these pictures illustrate:

18 pts.   a)   **N·x er··, et cae·· fulg···· l··· ser···**
                  in··· min··· sīd····.

        Nox erat, ·· caelō fulgēbat lūna serēnō

        inter minōra sīdera   .

20 pts.   b)   **Lūs···· s···s, ēd···· sat·· at···**
                bib····;
           t····s ab··· t··i ··t.

        Lūsistī satis, ēdistī satis atque bibistī;

        tempus abīre tibi est

                                     :

16 pts.   c) Dīv··· nāt··· de··· ag···; a·· hūm···
               aedif······ urb···.

Dīvīna nātūra dedit agrōs; ars hūmāna aedificāvit

urbēs   .

7) Write the review Basic Sentences which express approximately
    these thoughts:
    Sī deōs colimus, rem pūblicam custōdīmus.

12 pts.   a) Rel···· v··a ··· firm······· r··
               pūbl·····.

               Religiō vēra est firmāmentum reī pūblicae

               _____ .

           Rēgēs omnia vident atque audiunt.

10 pts.   b) Mult·· r···m aur·· atq·· oc····.

               Multae rēgum aurēs atque oculī

               _____ .

Total
158 pts.

EXTRA READINGS

17 pts.   a) **Sūmere vult piscēs cattus sed flūmen abhorret.** Med.

               The cat likes to catch fish but avoids the river[1]

               _____ .

13 pts.   b) **Mē lūmen, vōs umbra regit.** Sundial inscription

               Light rules me, but the shadows rule you[2]

               _____ .

Total
30 pts.

[1] If you want something, you usually have to go through some effort to get it.

[2] The sundial is under the influence of the sun, giver of light and life. We mortals, however, are under the constant threat of darkness, that is, death.

20 pts 1) Count from one to ten; remember the agreement of the adjective   2 points each word.
in the first three.

a)   _____ **ūnus**   **digitus**

b)   _____ **duo**   **digitī**

c)   _____ **trēs**   **digitī**

d)   _____ **quattuor**   **digitī**

e)   _____ **quīnque**   **digitī**

f)   _____ **sex**   **digitī**

g)   _____ **septem**   **digitī**

h)   _____ **octō**   **digitī**

i) _____ novem _____ digitī

j) _____ decem _____ digitī

2) Write the principal parts of the following verbs:

6 pts.   a) **trahō,** <u>**trahere**</u> , <u>**trāxī**</u> , <u>**tractus**</u> .

6 pts.   b) **aperiō,** <u>**aperīre**</u> , <u>**aperuī**</u> , <u>**apertus**</u> .

6 pts.   c) **quaerō,** <u>**quaerere**</u> , <u>**quaesīvī**</u> , <u>**quaesītus**</u> .

4 pts.   d) **maneō,** <u>**manēre**</u> , <u>**mānsī**</u> .

12 pts.   3) Write the conjugation of **laedō, laedere, laesī, laesus** in the #4 tense:

<u>**laeseram**</u>	<u>**laeserāmus**</u>
<u>**laeserās**</u>	<u>**laeserātis**</u>
<u>**laeserat**</u>	<u>**laeserant**</u>

6 pts.   4) Identify the tenses of the verbs in these changed Basic Sentences (**prīmī/secundī/tertiī/quārtī/quīntī**):

In ūnō saltū lepidē aprōs cēpī duōs.

a) " '**Cēpī**' est temporis <u>**quīntī**</u> ."

Certa mittēmus dum incerta petimus.

b) " '**Mittēmus**' est temporis <u>**tertiī**</u> ."

Caelō fulget lūna serēnō inter minōra sīdera.

c) " '**Fulget**' est temporis <u>**secundī**</u> ."

5) Write the following noun forms: Two points for each word.

2 pts.   a) "**Quid est 'lepus' in cāsū ablātīvō et numerō plūrālī?**" " <u>**leporibus**</u> ."

Latin: Level One Test for Unit Twenty-eight/102

2 pts.   b)   "Quid est 'lūx' in cāsū ablātīvō et numerō

singulārī?" "____lūce____."

2 pts.   c)   "Quid est 'pictūra' in cāsū genitīvō et

numerō plūrālī?" "____pictūrārum____."

2 pts.   d)   "Quid est 'aciēs' in cāsū ablātīvō et numerō

singulārī?" "____aciē____."

2 pts.   e)   "Quid est 'manus' in cāsū accūsātīvō et

numerō plūrālī?" "____manūs____."

10 pts.   6)   Give the new Basic Sentence which expresses approximately this thought:
Hodiē nōs omnēs vitia habēmus.
Qu·· fu····· vit··, mōr·· s····.

Quae fuerant vitia, mōrēs sunt _____.

32 pts.   7)   Fill in the missing letters:

La n g u ēbam, sed tū comit ā t u s prōtin u s

ad m ē

vēn i s t ī, cent u m, Symmach e,

dis c i p ulīs.

C e n t um mē tetig ē r e man ū s Aquil ō n e

gelātae.

Nōn hab u ī fēbr e m, Symmache, n u n c

hab e ō.

8 pts.   8)   Review Basic Sentence:
Hōrās nōn numerō, nisī serēnās.
"Quālia tempora tū in memoriā tenēre dēbēs?"

"Egō tempora ____serēna____ in memoriā tenēre

____dēbeō____."

Total
120 pts.

EXTRA READINGS

17 pts.   a) **Quī amat mē, amat et canem meum.** Anon.

Who loves me also loves my dog[1]

_____ .

[1]If you like me, you'll have to like my friends and relatives too.

9 pts.   b) **Dūcit amor patriae.** Motto of Lord Milford

Love of country guides (us)[2]

_____ .

[2](The person whose motto this is says that) patriotism is the most important thing in our lives.

Total
26 pts.

1) Write the synopses of the following verbs:

   a) **habeō, habēre, habuī, habitus** in the 2d singular (**Tū** as subject):

6 pts.   #1 **habēbās**   #2 **habēs**   #3 **habēbis**

6 pts.   #4 **habuerās**   #5 **habuistī**   #6 **habueris**

   b) **stō, stāre, stetī** in the 3d plural (**Virī** as subject):

6 pts.   #1 **stābant**   #2 **stant**   #3 **stābunt**

6 pts.   #4 **steterant**   #5 **stetērunt**   #6 **steterint**

2) Give the principal parts of the following verbs:

6 pts.   a) **faciō,**   facere   ,   fēcī   ,   factus   .

6 pts.   b) **pōnō,**   pōnere   ,   posuī   ,   positus   .

6 pts.   c) **tendō,**   tendere   ,   tetendī   ,   tēnsus   .

6 pts.   d) **rumpō,**   rumpere   ,   rūpī   ,   ruptus   .

4 pts.   e) **fugiō,**   fugere   ,   fūgī   .

12 pts. 3) Conjugate the irregular verb **volō** in the #2 tense:

volō	**volumus**
vīs	**vultis**
vult	**volunt**

2 pts. 4) a) **"Quid est 'aedificium' in cāsū accūsātīvō et numerō plūrālī?" "**   aedificia   **."**

2 pts.   b) **"Quid est 'hospes' in cāsū genitīvō et numerō singulārī?" "**   hospitis   **."**

2 pts.   c) **"Quid est 'carmen' in cāsū ablātīvō et numerō singulārī?" "**   Carmine   **."**

2 pts.   d) "Quid est 'sinus' in cāsū ablātīvō et

numerō singulārī?" "___Sinū___."

2 pts.   e) "Quid est 'libellus' in cāsū ablātīvō et

numerō plūrālī?" "___libellīs___."

22 pts.   5) Write the Basic Sentence which this picture illustrates: 2 points each word.
Dōn - - er - - fē - - x, mul - - - numer - - - -
amī - - - ;
temp - - - sī f - - - - nt nūb - - - , sōl - - er - - .

Dōnec eris fēlīx, multōs numerābis amīcōs; _____

tempora - - fuerint nūbila, sōlus eris _____

_____ .

6) Answer these questions on one of the new Readings:

4 pts.   a) "Quem auctōrem omnēs Rōmānī laudābant?"

"___Mārtiālem___."

8 pts.   b) Quid agēbat quīdam cui carmina Mārtiālis
nōn placēbant?"

"Rubēbat____, pallēbat____, stupēbat____,   Two of these verbs in any

ōderat____, ōscitābat_____."   combination are acceptable.
(Two verbs are enough.)

16 pts.   7) Complete the blanks on this new Reading:

Ho s p es erās nost r ī sem p e r, Matho,

Tīb u r tīnī.

Hocc em i s. Imp o s uī; r ū s t i b ī

vendo tuum.

4 pts. 8) Answer this question on a review Basic Sentence:
Vēritās vōs līberābit.
"Quālēs erimus sī vēritātem colimus?"

" **Līberī** ."

18 pts. 9) Complete the blanks in the review Reading:

Nūp er er a t medic u s , n u n c est

vespillo Diaul u s

Q u od v e s p i l l o fac i t , f ē c erat et

medicus.

Total
146 pts.

EXTRA READINGS

13 pts. a) **Glōriam quī sprēverit, vēram habēbit.** Livy 22.39.20

The person who has shunned glory will gain true glory[1]

.

[1]A person gains real fame, not by seeking publicity, but by trying to avoid it.

15 pts. b) **Cum fortūna perit, nūllus amīcus erit.** Med.

There will be no friends when fortune disappears[2]

.

[2]If your luck is bad, your friends will desert you.

Total
28 pts.

1) Here is a verb meaning "be on fire": **ardeō, ardēre, arsī.** Give a synopsis in the 2d person plural (**Vōs** as subject):

6 pts. #1 **ardēbātis** #2 **ardētis** #3 **ardēbitis**

6 pts. #4 **arserātis** #5 **arsistis** #6 **arseritis**

2) Give the principal parts of the following verbs:

6 pts. a) **vincō,** vincere , vīcī , victus .

6 pts. b) **capiō,** capere , cēpī , captus .

6 pts. c) **laxō,** laxāre , laxāvī , laxātus .

6 pts. d) **pingō,** pingere , pīnxī , pictus .

6 pts. e) **adjuvō,** adjuvāre , adjūvī , adjūtus .

2 pts. 3) a) "**Quid est 'successus' in cāsū genitīvō et numerō singulārī?**" " successūs ."

2 pts. b) "**Quid est 'gena' in cāsū nōminātīvō et numerō plūrālī?**" " genae ."

2 pts. c) "**Quid est 'color' in cāsū datīvō et numerō singulārī?**" " colōrī ."

2 pts. d) "**Quid est 'somnus' in cāsū ablātīvō et numerō singulārī?**" " somnō ."

2 pts. e) "**Quid est 'ōs' in cāsū accūsātīvō et numerō singulārī?**" " ōs ."

16 pts. 4) Fill in the blanks on this new Reading:

Quem recitās, meus est, Ō Fīdentīne, libellus;

sed male cum recitās, incipit esse tuus.

5) Lōtus nōbīscum est, hilaris cēnāvit, et īdem
    inventus māne est mortuus Andragorās.
    Tam subitae mortis causam, Faustīne, requīris?
    In somnīs medicum vīderat Hermocratēn.

(Reading #12)

Answer these questions on the new Reading:

4 pts.   a)   "Quāliter cēnāvit Andragorās?"

      "   Hilariter   ."

4 pts.   b)   "Quis quaerit, 'Cūr haec mors accidit?'?"

      "   Faustīnus   ."

4 pts.   c)   "Quālis erat mors Andragorae?"

      "   Subita   ."

4 pts.   d)   "Cujus amīcus erat Andragorās?"

      "   Mārtiālis (Faustīnī)   ."

32 pts.   6)   Fill in the blanks on this Review Reading:

     Si quandō leporem mittis, mihi,

     Gellia, dīcis,

     "Formōsus septem, Mārce, diēbus

     eris."

     Si nōn dērīdēs, sī vērum, lūx mea,

     nārrās

     ēdistī numquam, Gellia, tū

     leporem.

7)   Write the review Basic Sentences which these pictures illustrate:

12 pts.   a)   - -od   n - -   ded - -   For - - - -   n - -   ēri - - - .

Quod nōn dedit Fortūna nōn ēripit   .

10 pts.   b)   **Lin · · a   m · · ī   p · · s   pes · · · ·   ser · · ·**

Lingua malī pars pessima servī _____ .

20 pts.   c)   **J · · que   quiēsc · · · · ·   vō · · ·   hom · · · · · · ·**
                 can · · · · ·
      l · · · que   noct · · · · ·   al · ·   reg · · · ·   eq · · · ·

Jamque quiēscēbant vōcēs hominumque canumque

lūnaque nocturnōs alta regēbat equōs _____ .

Total
158 pts.

EXTRA READINGS

35 pts.   a)   **In idem flūmen bis dēscendimus et nōn dēscendimus. Manet enim idem flūminis nōmen; aqua trānsmissa est.** Seneca, _Ep._ 58.23

We do and we do not step twice into the same river. For

the name of the river stays the same, but the water passes

by.[1] _____

_____ .

[1]Because of the fact that you have changed, you are not the same person you were ten years ago even though you are legally the same person.

17 pts.   b)   **Bis vincit quī sē vincit in victōriā.** Publilius Syrus

Who conquers himself in victory wins a double victory[2]

_____ .

[2]The first victory is to defeat someone else. The second victory is to be able to control yourself and not to let the victory spoil you.

Total
52 pts.

CONVERSION TABLES FOR TESTS

CONVERSION TABLES FOR TESTS

UNIT #2

Raw Score	%
48	100
47	98
46	96
45	94
44	92
43	90
42	88
41	86
40	84
39	81
38	79
37	77
36	75
35	73
34	71
33	69
32	67
31	65
30	63
29	61
28	59

UNIT #3

Raw Score	%
44	100
43	98
42	96
41	93
40	91
39	89
38	86
37	84
36	82
35	80
34	77
33	75
32	73
31	71
30	68
29	66
28	64
27	62
26	59

UNIT #4

Raw Score	%
60	100
59	99
58	97
57	95
56	93
55	92
54	90
53	88
52	87
51	85
50	83
49	82
48	80
47	78
46	77
45	75
44	74
43	72
42	70
41	68
40	67
39	65
38	64
37	62
36	60

UNIT #5		UNIT #6		UNIT #7	
Raw Score	%	Raw Score	%	Raw Score	%
86	100	66	100	80	100
85	99	65	99	79	99
84	98	64	97	78	98
83	97	63	96	77	96
82	96	62	94	76	95
81	94	61	93	75	94
80	93	60	91	74	93
79	92	59	90	73	91
78	91	58	88	72	90
77	90	57	87	71	89
76	89	56	85	70	88
75	87	55	84	69	86
74	86	54	82	68	85
73	85	53	81	67	84
72	84	52	79	66	83
71	83	51	78	65	81
70	82	50	76	64	80
69	80	49	75	63	79
68	79	48	73	62	78
67	78	47	71	61	76
66	77	46	70	60	75
65	76	45	68	59	74
64	75	44	67	58	73
63	73	43	65	57	71
62	72	42	64	56	70
61	71	41	62	55	69
60	70	40	61	54	68
59	69			53	66
58	68			52	65
57	67			51	64
56	65			50	63
55	64			49	61
54	63			48	60
53	62				
52	61				
51	60				

UNIT #8		UNIT #9		UNIT #10	
Raw Score	%	Raw Score	%	Raw Score	%
118	100	80	100	102	100
117	99	79	99	101	99
116	98	78	98	100	98
115	97	77	96	99	97
114	97	76	95	98	96
113	96	75	94	97	95
112	95	74	93	96	94
111	94	73	91	95	93
110	93	72	90	94	92
109	93	71	89	93	91
108	92	70	88	92	90
107	91	69	86	91	89
106	90	68	85	90	88
105	89	67	84	89	87
104	88	66	83	88	86
103	87	65	81	87	85
102	86	64	80	86	84
101	86	63	79	85	83
100	85	62	78	84	82
99	84	61	76	83	81
98	83	60	75	82	80
97	82	59	74	81	80
96	81	58	73	80	79
95	81	57	71	79	78
94	80	56	70	78	77
93	79	55	69	77	76
92	78	54	68	76	75
91	77	53	66	75	74
90	76	52	65	74	73
89	76	51	64	73	72
88	75	50	63	72	71
87	74	49	61	71	70
86	73	48	60	70	69
85	72			69	68
84	71			68	67
83	71			67	66
82	70			66	65
81	69			65	64
80	68			64	63
79	67			63	62
78	66			62	61
77	65			61	60
76	65				
75	64				
74	63				
73	62				
72	61				
71	60				

UNIT #11		UNIT #12		UNIT #13	
Raw Score	%	Raw Score	%	Raw Score	%
78	100	68	100	158	100
77	99	67	99	157	100
76	98	66	97	156	99
75	96	65	96	155	98
74	95	64	94	154	98
73	94	63	93	153	97
72	92	62	91	152	96
71	91	61	90	151	96
70	90	60	88	150	95
69	89	59	87	149	94
68	87	58	85	148	94
67	86	57	84	147	93
66	85	56	82	146	92
65	83	55	81	145	92
64	82	54	79	144	91
63	81	53	78	143	90
62	80	52	76	142	90
61	78	51	75	141	89
60	77	50	74	140	89
59	76	49	72	139	88
58	75	48	71	138	87
57	73	47	69	137	87
56	72	46	68	136	86
55	71	45	66	135	85
54	69	44	65	134	85
53	68	43	63	133	84
52	67	42	62	132	84
51	66	41	60	131	83
50	64			130	82
49	63			129	82
48	62			128	81
47	60			127	80
				126	80
				125	79
				124	79
				123	78
				122	77
				121	77
				120	76
				119	75
				118	75
				117	74
				116	73
				115	73
				114	72
				113	72
				112	71
				111	70

		UNIT #14		UNIT #15	
		Raw Score	%	Raw Score	%
110	70	116	100	202	100
109	69	115	99	201	100
108	68	114	99	200	100
107	68	113	98	199	99
106	67	112	97	198	99
105	66	111	96	197	98
104	66	110	95	196	98
103	65	109	94	195	97
102	65	108	93	194	97
101	64	107	92	193	96
100	63	106	91	192	96
99	63	105	90	191	95
98	62	104	90	190	95
97	61	103	89	189	94
96	61	102	88	188	94
95	60	101	87	187	93
		100	86	186	93
		99	86	185	92
		98	85	184	92
		97	84	183	91
		96	83	182	91
		95	82	181	90
		94	81	180	90
		93	80	179	89
		92	80	178	89
		91	79	177	88
		90	78	176	88
		89	77	175	87
		88	76	174	87
		87	75	173	86
		86	74	172	86
		85	73	171	85
		84	73	170	85
		83	72	169	84
		82	71	168	84
		81	70	167	83
		80	69	166	83
		79	68	165	82
		78	67	164	82
		77	67	163	81
		76	66	162	81
		75	65	161	80
		74	64	160	80
		73	63	159	79
		72	62	158	79
		71	61	157	78
		70	60	156	78
				155	77

UNIT #16

		Raw Score	%
154	77	108	100
153	76	107	99
152	76	106	98
151	75	105	97
150	75	104	96
149	74	103	95
148	74	102	94
147	73	101	94
146	73	100	93
145	72	99	92
144	72	98	91
143	71	97	90
142	71	96	89
141	70	95	88
140	70	94	87
139	69	93	86
138	69	92	85
137	68	91	85
136	68	90	84
135	67	89	83
134	67	88	82
133	66	87	81
132	66	86	80
131	65	85	79
130	65	84	78
129	64	83	77
128	64	82	76
127	63	81	75
126	63	80	74
125	62	79	73
124	62	78	72
123	61	77	71
122	61	76	71
121	60	75	70
120	60	74	69
		73	68
		72	67
		71	66
		70	65
		69	64
		68	63
		67	62
		66	61
		65	60

UNIT #17

Raw Score	%
122	100
121	99
120	98
119	98
118	97
117	96
116	95
115	94
114	94
113	93
112	92
111	91
110	90
109	89
108	89
107	88
106	87
105	86
104	85
103	85
102	84
101	83
100	82
99	81
98	80
97	79
96	79
95	78
94	77
93	76
92	75
91	75
90	74
89	73
88	72
87	71
86	71
85	70
84	69
83	68
82	67
81	66
80	66
79	65
78	64
77	63
76	62
75	62
74	61
73	60

UNIT #18

Raw Score	%
188	100
187	100
186	99
185	99
184	98
183	97
182	97
181	96
180	96
179	95
178	95
177	94
176	94
175	93
174	93
173	92
172	92
171	91
170	91
169	90
168	90
167	89
166	88
165	88
164	87
163	87
162	86
161	86
160	85
159	85
158	84
157	84
156	83
155	83
154	82
153	82
152	81
151	81
150	80
149	79
148	79
147	78
146	78
145	77
144	77
143	76
142	76
141	75
140	75
139	74
138	74
137	73
136	72
135	72
134	71
133	71
132	70
131	70
130	69
129	69
128	68
127	68
126	67
125	67
124	66
123	66
122	65
121	65
120	64
119	63
118	63
117	62
116	62
115	61
114	61
113	60

UNIT #19

Raw Score	%
197	100
196	100
195	99
194	99
193	98
192	98
191	97
190	97
189	96
188	96
187	95
186	95
185	94
184	94
183	93
182	92
181	92
180	91
179	91
178	90
177	90
176	89
175	89
174	88
173	88
172	87
171	87
170	86
169	86
168	85
167	85
166	84
165	84
164	83
163	83
162	82
161	82
160	81
159	81
158	80
157	80
156	79
155	79
154	78
153	78
152	77
151	77
150	76

UNIT #20

		Raw Score	%
149	76	104	100
148	75	103	99
147	75	102	98
146	74	101	97
145	74	100	96
144	73	99	95
143	73	98	94
142	72	97	93
141	72	96	92
140	71	95	91
139	71	94	90
138	70	93	90
137	70	92	89
136	69	91	88
135	69	90	87
134	68	89	86
133	68	88	85
132	67	87	84
131	67	86	83
130	66	85	82
129	66	84	81
128	65	83	80
127	64	82	79
126	64	81	78
125	63	80	77
124	63	79	76
123	62	78	75
122	62	77	74
121	61	76	73
120	61	75	72
119	60	74	71
118	60	73	70
		72	69
		71	68
		70	67
		69	66
		68	65
		67	64
		66	63
		65	62
		64	62
		63	61
		62	60

UNIT #21

Raw Score	%
128	100
127	99
126	98
125	98
124	97
123	96
122	95
121	95
120	94
119	93
118	92
117	92
116	91
115	90
114	89
113	88
112	88
111	87
110	86
109	85
108	84
107	84
106	83
105	82
104	81
103	81
102	80
101	79
100	78
99	77
98	77
97	76
96	75
95	74
94	74
93	73
92	72
91	71
90	70
89	70
88	69
87	68
86	67
85	66
84	66
83	65
82	64
81	63

UNIT #22

Raw Score	%				
		146	100	98	67
80	63	145	99	97	67
79	62	144	99	96	66
78	61	143	98	95	65
77	60	142	97	94	64
		141	97	93	64
		140	96	92	63
		139	95	91	62
		138	95	90	62
		137	94	89	61
		136	93	88	60
		135	92	87	60
		134	92		
		133	91		
		132	90		
		131	90		
		130	89		
		129	88		
		128	88		
		127	87		
		126	86		
		125	86		
		124	85		
		123	84		
		122	84		
		121	83		
		120	82		
		119	82		
		118	81		
		117	80		
		116	79		
		115	79		
		114	78		
		113	77		
		112	77		
		111	76		
		110	75		
		109	75		
		108	74		
		107	73		
		106	73		
		105	72		
		104	71		
		103	71		
		102	70		
		101	69		
		100	69		
		99	68		

Raw Score	%	Raw Score	%	Raw Score	%
167	100	119	71	124	100
166	99	118	71	123	99
165	99	117	70	122	98
164	98	116	69	121	98
163	98	115	69	120	97
162	97	114	68	119	96
161	96	113	68	118	95
160	96	112	67	117	94
159	95	111	66	116	94
158	95	110	66	115	93
157	94	109	65	114	92
156	93	108	65	113	91
155	93	107	64	112	90
154	92	106	63	111	90
153	92	105	63	110	89
152	91	104	62	109	88
151	90	103	62	108	87
150	90	102	61	107	86
149	89	101	60	106	86
148	89	100	60	105	85
147	88			104	84
146	87			103	83
145	87			102	82
144	86			101	82
143	86			100	81
142	85			99	80
141	84			98	79
140	84			97	78
139	83			96	78
138	83			95	77
137	82			94	76
136	81			93	75
135	81			92	74
134	80			91	73
133	80			90	73
132	79			89	72
131	78			88	71
130	78			87	70
129	77			86	69
128	77			85	69
127	76			84	68
126	75			83	67
125	75			82	66
124	74			81	65
123	74			80	65
122	73			79	64
121	72			78	63
120	72			77	62

UNIT #25

		Raw Score	%		
76	61	128	100	81	63
75	61	127	99	80	63
74	60	126	98	79	62
		125	98	78	61
		124	97	77	60
		123	96		
		122	95		
		121	95		
		120	94		
		119	93		
		118	92		
		117	92		
		116	91		
		115	90		
		114	89		
		113	88		
		112	88		
		111	87		
		110	86		
		109	85		
		108	84		
		107	84		
		106	83		
		105	82		
		104	81		
		103	81		
		102	80		
		101	79		
		100	78		
		99	77		
		98	77		
		97	76		
		96	75		
		95	74		
		94	74		
		93	73		
		92	72		
		91	71		
		90	70		
		89	70		
		88	69		
		87	68		
		86	67		
		85	66		
		84	66		
		83	65		
		82	64		

UNIT #26

Raw Score	%
142	100
141	99
140	99
139	98
138	97
137	97
136	96
135	95
134	94
133	94
132	93
131	92
130	92
129	91
128	90
127	90
126	89
125	88
124	87
123	87
122	86
121	85
120	85
119	84
118	83
117	82
116	82
115	81
114	80
113	80
112	79
111	78
110	78
109	77
108	76
107	75
106	75
105	74
104	73
103	73
102	72
101	71
100	71
99	70
98	69
97	68
96	68
95	67

94	66
93	66
92	65
91	64
90	63
89	63
88	62
87	61
86	61
85	60

UNIT #27

Raw Score	%
158	100
157	100
156	99
155	98
154	98
153	97
152	96
151	96
150	95
149	94
148	94
147	93
146	92
145	92
144	91
143	90
142	90
141	89
140	89
139	88
138	87
137	87
136	86
135	85
134	85
133	84
132	84
131	83
130	82
129	82
128	81
127	80
126	80
125	79
124	79
123	78
122	77
121	77
120	76
119	75
118	75
117	74
116	73
115	73
114	72
113	72
112	71
111	70

Raw Score	%
110	70
109	69
108	68
107	68
106	67
105	66
104	66
103	65
102	65
101	64
100	63
99	63
98	62
97	61
96	61
95	60

UNIT #28

Raw Score	%
120	100
119	99
118	99
117	98
116	97
115	96
114	95
113	94
112	93
111	92
110	92
109	91
108	90
107	89
106	88
105	87
104	87
103	86
102	85
101	84
100	83
99	82
98	82
97	81
96	80
95	79
94	78
93	77
92	77
91	76
90	75
89	74
88	74
87	73
86	72
85	71
84	70
83	69
82	68
81	67
80	67
79	66
78	65
77	64
76	64
75	63
74	62
73	61
72	60

UNIT #29

Raw Score	%
146	100
145	99
144	99
143	98
142	97
141	97
140	96
139	95
138	95
137	94
136	93
135	92
134	92
133	91
132	90
131	90
130	89
129	88
128	88
127	87
126	86
125	86
124	85
123	84
122	84
121	83
120	82
119	82
118	81
117	80
116	79
115	79
114	78
113	77
112	77
111	76
110	75
109	75
108	74
107	73
106	73
105	72
104	71
103	71
102	70
101	69
100	69
99	68
98	67

UNIT #30

		Raw Score	%		
97	67	158	100	110	70
96	66	157	100	109	69
95	65	156	99	108	68
94	64	155	98	107	68
93	64	154	98	106	67
92	63	153	97	105	66
91	62	152	96	104	66
90	62	151	96	103	65
89	61	150	95	102	65
88	60	149	94	101	64
87	60	148	94	100	63
		147	93	99	63
		146	92	98	62
		145	92	97	61
		144	91	96	61
		143	90	95	60
		142	90		
		141	89		
		140	89		
		139	88		
		138	87		
		137	87		
		136	86		
		135	85		
		134	85		
		133	84		
		132	84		
		131	83		
		130	82		
		129	82		
		128	81		
		127	80		
		126	80		
		125	79		
		124	79		
		123	78		
		122	77		
		121	77		
		120	76		
		119	75		
		118	75		
		117	74		
		116	73		
		115	73		
		114	72		
		113	72		
		112	71		
		111	70		

Latin: Level One Conversion Tables/128

COMPONENTS OF THE *ARTES LATINAE* COURSE

ARTES LATINAE
by Waldo Sweet

Published by Bolchazy-Carducci Publishers, Inc.

Originally published by Encyclopaedia Brittannica Educational Corporation

CD-ROM FORMAT
With Three Pronunciations

Each disk is the equivalent of Books 1 & 2 and the cassettes in the traditional format.

CD-ROM package includes the following materials:
- Manual
- TM Graded Reader
- Unit Test Booklet
- Graded Reader
- Reference Notebook
- Unit Test Guide

This is as practical and easy to use as any language program I have ever encountered.
–John A. Jackson, *International Congress on Medieval Studies Conferee*

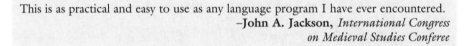

TRADITIONAL FORMAT
Traditional package includes the following materials:

Level I	*Level II*
Phase I: #0101 #290-5, Student Text, Book I #293-X, Unit Test Booklet (consumable) #295-6, Reference Notebook (consumable) #298-0, Guide to Unit Tests Three Audio Cassette Tapes (units 1–2: #359-6, 3–4: #360-X, 5–6: #361-8)	**Phase I: #0201** #299-9, Student Text, Book I #301-4, Unit Test Booklet (consumable) #306-5, Guide to Unit Tests #303-0, Reference Notebook (consumable) #304-9, Teacher's Manual Two Audio Cassette Tapes (units 1–2: #375-8, 3–4: #376-6)
Phase II: #0102 #294-8, Graded Reader (*Lectiones Primae*) #297-2, TM Graded Reader #296-4, Teachers Manual Four Audio Cassette Tapes (units 7–8: #362-6, 9–10: #363-4, 11–12: #364-2, 13–14: #365-0)	**Phase II: #0202** #302-2, Graded Reader (*Lectiones Secundae*) #305-7, TM Graded Reader Four Audio Cassette Tapes (units 5–6: #377-4, 7–8: #378-2, 9–10: #379-0, 11–12: #380-4)
Phase III: #0103 #292-1, Student Text Book II Four Audio Cassette Tapes (units 15–16: #366-9, 17–18: #367-7, 19–20: #368-5, 21–22: #369-3)	**Phase III: #0203** #300-6, Student Text, Book II Three Audio Cassette Tapes (units 13–14: #382-0, 15–16: #383-9, 17–18: #384-7)
Phase IV: #0104 Four Audio Cassettes Tapes (units 23–24: #370-7, 25–26: #371-5, 27–28: #372-3, 29–30: 373-1)	**Phase IV: #0204** Three Audio Cassette Tapes (units 19–20: #385-5, 21–22: #386-3, 23–24: #387-1)

BOLCHAZY-CARDUCCI PUBLISHERS, INC.
WWW.ARTESLATINAE.COM